Anthony Neilson
Plays: 1

Normal, Penetrator, Year of the Family
The Night Before Christmas, The Censor

Normal: 'a tight, powerful three-hander ... achieved with a sense of discipline and thematic energy.' *Guardian*

Penetrator: 'This is one of the blackest, funniest and most shocking comedy dramas you will ever see.' *Sunday Times*

Year of the Family: 'His writing is as tight and courageous as ever ... highly recommended for those who like to think.' *What's On*

The Night Before Christmas: 'It is a smutty, dangerously funny but ultimately warm-hearted cri de coeur against the Christmas industry.' *Stage*

The Censor: 'This is a profound and tragic vision of humanity at its bare, forked basics.' *Evening Standard*

Anthony Neilson was born and raised in Scotland. He has been thrown out of, banned from and ostracised by some of the country's foremost institutions; also, the Hampstead Theatre. He lives alone with his wife and ten children.

D0723563

Methuen Contemporary Dramatists

include

Peter Barnes (three volumes)
Sebastian Barry
Edward Bond (six volumes)
Howard Brenton
  (two volumes)
Richard Cameron
Jim Cartwright
Caryl Churchill (two volumes)
Sarah Daniels (two volumes)
David Edgar (three volumes)
Dario Fo (two volumes)
Michael Frayn (two volumes)
Peter Handke
Jonathan Harvey
Declan Hughes
Terry Johnson
Bernard-Marie Koltès
Doug Lucie
David Mamet (three volumes)

Anthony Minghella
  (two volumes)
Tom Murphy (four volumes)
Phyllis Nagy
Peter Nichols (two volumes)
Philip Osment
Louise Page
Stephen Poliakoff
  (three volumes)
Christina Reid
Philip Ridley
Willy Russell
Ntozake Shange
Sam Shepard (two volumes)
David Storey (three volumes)
Sue Townsend
Michel Vinaver (two volumes)
Michael Wilcox

ANTHONY NEILSON

Plays: 1

Normal
Penetrator
The Year of the Family
The Night Before Christmas
The Censor

Methuen Drama

METHUEN CONTEMPORARY DRAMATISTS

2 4 6 8 10 9 7 5 3

The right of Anthony Neilson to be identified as the author of this work has been asserted by him in accordance with the Copyright, Designs and Patents Act, 1988

This collection first published in Great Britain in 1998
by Methuen Drama
215 Vauxhall Bridge Road
London SW1V 1EJ

Methuen Publishing Ltd Reg No. 3543167

Normal copyright © 1998 by Anthony Neilson
Penetrator copyright © 1998 by Anthony Neilson
Year of the Family copyright © 1998 by Anthony Neilson
The Night Before Christmas copyright © 1998 by Anthony Neilson
The Censor first published in 1997 as a Methuen Modern Play
copyright © 1997 by Anthony Neilson

This collection copyright © 1998 by Anthony Neilson
Introduction copyright © 1998 by Anthony Neilson

Lines from 'The Trail of the Lonesome Pine': Words by Ballard MacDonald, Music by Harry Carroll, Copyright © 1913, Renewed, Shapiro, Bernstein & Co. Inc. New York, NY. International Copyright secured. All Rights Reserved.

A CIP catalogue record for this book
is available from the British Library

ISBN 0–413–72460–3

Typeset by Deltatype Ltd, Birkenhead, Merseyside
Printed and bound in Great Britain by
Cox & Wyman Ltd, Reading, Berkshire

Caution

All rights whatsoever in this play are strictly reserved and application for performance, etc., should be made before rehearsals begin to Hamilton Asper Management, Ground Floor, 24 Hanway Street, London W1P 9DD. No performance may be given unless a licence has been obtained.

This book is sold subject to the condition that it shall not, by way of trade or otherwise, be lent, resold, hired out or otherwise circulated without the publisher's prior consent in any form of binding or cover other than that in which it is published and without a similar condition being imposed on the subsequent purchaser.

Contents

Chronology   vii

Introduction   ix

NORMAL   1

PENETRATOR   59

YEAR OF THE FAMILY   121

THE NIGHT BEFORE CHRISTMAS   195

THE CENSOR   243

Anthony Neilson:
A Chronology

1988 The Colours Of The King's Rose (*radio play*)

1990 Welfare My Lovely

1990 A Fluttering Of Wings (*radio play*)

1991 Normal

1992 Deeper Still (*short film*)

1993 Penetrator

1994 Year Of The Family

1995 Heredity

1995 Jeffrey Dahmer Is Unwell (*co-written with Alan Francis and Mike Hayley*)

1995 The Night Before Christmas

1996 Hooverbag

1997 Twisted (*radio play*)

1997 The Censor

Introduction

Playwriting is one of those things that is both undervalued and overestimated.

I don't think I need to explain the former. But on the rare occasions when I teach, I'm always surprised at how the playwright is perceived as a kind of politician without allegiance. Now there are some very good writers for whom you could make exactly that claim but it's a burdensome notion for someone starting out. When I would ask the students, for example, what ideas they had, they would almost always respond in themes. They wanted to write plays about racism, about homelessness, about the erosion of democracy. They wanted to 'say something' and this was seen as a fundamental requirement of a play: that it should 'say something'.

Of course these same students were usually blocked and unproductive. They had their theme all right, but no idea of how to proceed, because they were unwilling to accept that a playwright is no more and no less than a *storyteller* – a direct descendant of that person that would sit in the village square and tell fairy tales to children. When confronted with this many students were amazingly resistant, disappointed even, as if a narrative was – in and of itself – somehow unadventurous, old-fashioned. 'Tell a *story*,' I would bang on, 'and the themes will take care of themselves.'

The story is the route by which your subconscious finds expression in the real world. Preoccupying yourself with the mechanics of a narrative frees you from your ego and allows something more truthful to come through. And when it is done, it will surely 'say something', because character is action: the choices you make for your characters will reflect your personality, your take on the world, honestly and without cliché. In short, you will produce a truly dynamic thing: a play that speaks both to its audience and its creator. A two-way dialogue of creation and response.

Of course, in theatre especially, there are those that search tirelessly for an alternative to narrative. Such a quest is laudable but, in my experience, doomed to failure. By dint of the fact that everything begins and ends, the denial of narrative is a denial of life. (For a fuller illustration of this, I'd point you to David Mamet's essay 'Countercultural Architecture and Dramatic Structure', which hits the nail on the head.) If someone ever finds a better way, I'll be the first to rejoice. But until they do, I'd recommend that all writers concentrate on perfecting their storytelling abilities – which is a lifetime's work in itself.

To reiterate then: the playwright is the natural descendant of the village storyteller. Why the playwright and not, say, the novelist? By the very fact that the nature of theatre is ephemeral. When a production of a play is over, it lives on only in the memory of its audience. That's the absolute beauty of theatre and that's why it's only in theatre that we find a form that truly captures the impression of our fragile and transient lives.

And that's why, ultimately, I find myself somewhat uncomfortable about this little volume. Publishing plays seems contradictory, reductive. I've a feeling that – like holiday snaps and marriage vidoes – it all stems from our fear of impermanence, and finally of death. Because embracing that means we have to weave a little pain in with all our joys. It also means we have to acknowledge a certain joy in all our pain. I'm not sure which is harder.

I hope, at least, that you're reading this because you want to produce one of these plays. They're not meant to sit on the page. They were not created solely by me, but each by a team of friends and colleagues, and what you really have here is a transcript of our experiences. I would be very happy if you could make them experiences and memories of your own.

To that end, I'd implore you not to be reverent. Change them as you see fit in whatever time and place you are. Make them better – God knows there's opportunity for that – or better yet, replace my flaws with your own. Above all, make them live and breathe.

I'd just like to end with a line from a (not very good) radio play. Still, if you'll excuse the indulgence, I think it sums up the spirit in which these plays were written: 'And what are we but short, sad stories written by the world, and that itself a story, wrote by who knows what?'

As with everything, these plays are dedicated to the people I love. They know (I hope) who they are.

Normal

Normal was first performed at the Pleasance Theatre, Edinburgh, on 7 August 1991 and transferred to the Finborough Theatre, London, on 1 October 1991. The cast was as follows:

Justus Wehner	Craig Edwards
Peter Kurten	Jon Sotherton
Frau Kurten	Juliet Prew

Directed by Anthony Neilson
Designed by Michael T. Roberts

Characters

Justus Wehner
Peter Kurten
Frau Kurten

I: 1952

Spotlight picks out **Wehner**.

Wehner   Of course rarely a day had passed that I had
   not thought of him.
But time had left only the memory
of a memory
and it seemed to me that the chill he had placed in my
   soul
had finally thawed.
I had not reckoned on feeling that chill again so soon
and least of all here: in an amusement arcade,
many miles from my homeland.

Lights come up on the rest of the stage. **Kurten** *stands in an
unnaturally stiff pose, his back to the audience, stage left. He is at the
foot of some twisted steps which lead to the back rostra. Atop the
rostra a swan has risen, its wings outstretched. In his hand,* **Kurten**
holds a pair of ludicrously-oversized scissors.

Wehner   It looked a harmless enough thing;
a glass case which,
surrounded as it was by children,
I took at first for a sweet-dispenser of some kind.
Two of those children were my own,
eager to feed it a coin and
God forgive me
I gave them that coin
and let the infernal thing be activated.

Kurten *jerks into life. His scissor arm twitches and he begins his
slow clockwork walk up the stairs.*

Wehner   It was only then that I understood the true
nature of the machine. My fascinated babes could not have
known what it meant for me.
For all mankind.
I suppose I should have dragged them away but such was
   my
horror

that I could only stand there and watch him;
the monster
the ripper
Peter
Watch him mount the steps —

Kurten *reaches the top step. He is facing the swan. His scissor arm slowly rises.*

Wehner   Watch him raise his blades of polished steel and remember
how they had spoken of it in whispers;
that once,
having found no victim in the Hofgarten,
he had

Kurten*'s scissor arm reaches its optimum arc, hovers there and then:*

Wehner   he had
cut —

The scissors come down. The lights snap out.

II: Refrain

Light comes up. We see **Kurten** *in silhouette. He is looking up at the swan. We hear the voice of* **Kurten***'s wife, and as we do the swan sinks slowly back down behind the stage.*

Frau Kurten   Peter?
Peter, what is it that's happened?
Peter, what have you done this time?
The police were looking for you
Is it serious?
What is it that's happened, Peter?
Peter, what have you *done*?

III: A waltz back through time

Lights up on **Wehner**.

Wehner What is most ironic is that I was given the case
as a gift
by my elders in the legal establishment.
Still in my twenties, I was their most prided and precocious
son and it's true
I knew everything of the law.
Little of life
and less of love
But I knew everything of the law.
The year was 1931.

Music. A Weillian nightmare waltz. **Wehner** *exits only to re-enter
waltzing with a period dress-dummy. As he waltzes:*

Five million people were unemployed
the German economy was in ruins
and our eighty-four-year-old President sinking into senility.
Little wonder that the capture of the Dusseldorf Ripper was
so seized upon by both press and public.
Between February 1929 and May of 1930, eight lives had
been taken by Peter Kurten.
And so, for fifteen months,
a black fog of fear had been settled on Dusseldorf
and there was no escape from it;
if you opened your window
it crept into your home.
All manner of means were employed in the hunt for the
killer, from graphology to clairvoyance.
They even dressed a mannequin as one of his victims and
had a man waltz with her in various dance-halls.
The hope was that someone might remember her last
dancing
partner.

Music fades. The waltz dies and **Wehner** *stands there with the
dummy in his arms. A memory flickers across his eyes.*

I think I dreamt of that at the time.

Then he lifts the dummy into a horizontal position almost as if carrying a corpse.

So that was my gift:
I was to be his defence lawyer.
It was a prestigious case, and in those still liberal times it seemed that it might easily be won.
After all, I did not have to prove him innocent,
Just insane.
And he was surely that.

Wehner *lays the dummy down and kneels over it.*

But I knew little of life.

He covers the dummy with a cloth, takes one last look at her and then covers over her face.

And less
Of love.

The light fades.

IV: Refrain 2

Light comes up on **Kurten** *again as in Scene II. Again we hear the voice of* **Kurten**'s *wife.*

Frau Kurten   Peter?

V: First encounter with the ripper/1931

Lights change. **Wehner** *looks up at* **Kurten** *atop the rostra.* **Kurten**'s *back is still to the audience.*

Wehner   Peter Kurten?

Kurten *turns slowly to face him. He is immaculately dressed, his cheeks just slightly rouged. He is a handsome man, in his late forties.*

Wehner   I'm your lawyer. Dr Wehner.

Kurten *slowly walks down the steps gazing intensely at* **Wehner**, *who instinctively backs away. They regard each other for some time.*

Kurten   I wonder –
perhaps you could tell me –
is my hair unkempt?

Wehner *looks puzzled.*

Kurten   There are no mirrors here.
Could you tell me?

Wehner   Your hair seems fine.

Kurten   Honestly?

Wehner *(pause)*   Honestly.

Kurten *(relieved)*   I'm afraid I can't offer you much in the
way of refreshment.
But I could have some water sent in.
Perhaps some water?

Wehner *(pause)*   No. Thank you. I'd rather get down to
business.

Kurten   Of course.
I must admit I was expecting
an older man.

Wehner   I think you'll find me quite capable, Mr Kurten.

Kurten   Oh I don't doubt that.
I'm already impressed by your composure
Considering that I am
Who I am.

Wehner *(pause)*   You're still a human being, Mr Kurten.
Whatever you've done.

Kurten *regards him, enchanted.*

Kurten   So.
What goes on in the world
In our beleagured country?
I am also denied the papers you see
They think that I might morbidly pour over the details of
my case.

Wehner (*pause*)   Would you?

Kurten *does not answer.*

Wehner   We must get on.

Kurten   You intend to prove that I am insane.

Wehner   Are you?

Kurten   What do you think?

Wehner   I think that you must be.

Kurten   You hope that I am.

Wehner   I'm trying to save your life.

Kurten   My dear young boy.

Wehner   They'll execute you, Mr Kurten.
Doesn't that frighten you?

Kurten   Why should I be afraid?
I am what they fear.

Pause. **Wehner** *consults his documents.*

Wehner   You were born in Mulheim in 1883, third child
of thirteen. A large family.

Kurten   And we all lived in one room.

Wehner   Tell me about your family.

Kurten   Family.
My mother was an average woman of unexceptional stock.
My grandfather was a thief, a simpleton and a violent
alcoholic.
As were his children.

Wehner   Your father too?

Kurten   I can't recall him stealing anything.

Wehner   But he was
violent?

Kurten   Oh yes.
Spare the rod
Spoil the child.

Wehner   Did you respect him for it?

Kurten   I had little choice in the matter.

Wehner (*pause*)   Tell me about your sisters.

Kurten   Unattractive mostly, save one
who had the roundest of bottoms and the fullest of mouths.
That was the one thing that my father and I agreed upon.

Wehner   Your father was imprisoned for attempting to
rape one of his daughters.
Was that her?

Kurten *does not answer.*

Wehner   Did you also attempt to rape her?

Kurten   Rape?
Living in one room, Dr Wehner, there is little space for
Inhibition.
Most of my sisters made advances towards me
and only on that one occasion did I reciprocate.
Are you a virgin, Dr Wehner?

Wehner *is taken aback by this.*

Kurten   Did your parents tell you what goes where?
Did you all undress in separate rooms?
Were you ashamed when you got hair on your balls?

Wehner   Mr Kurten –

Kurten   Were you frightened by the noises that came
from their room?
Did you ever see your mother's cunt?

Wehner   That's enough!!

A long pause.

I'm good at my job, Mr Kurten.

Kurten (*pause*)   You see, Dr Wehner
When my father wanted to
take my mother he took her
In that room
In full view of us all.
That was my family.
I was never
an innocent.

Wehner *hangs his head in pity.*

Kurten   Don't.
On the whole it was to my advantage.
There is no place for innocence in this world.

VI: First letter home

Lights on **Wehner** *alone.*

Wehner   Dusseldorf, March 1931
Dear Mama
Dear Papa
As you must know, I have been appointed defence in the
Ripper case
and today I met Kurten face to face.
I felt strangely unafraid
But it is just as you guessed;
he has indeed endured an insufferable upbringing.
I think we have an excellent case and I know already the
angle I intend to use.
Victory would be certain
were it not for the rather worrisome change I detect in the
air.
I'm counting on you and your colleagues in the
Humanitarian League to put pressure on those that count.
I know you plan to send a delegation, will you be part of
it? I haven't see you
in such a long time.
Must go now
My love to all

Your son
Justus.
P.S.
Have you heard anything of Eva? She must be all grown
up now. Ask her to write to me should you see her.
For some reason, our summers together have returned to
my mind.

VII: Horror's coin

Lights up on rest of stage as in Scene V.

Kurten   Dr Wehner?

Wehner *turns, startled.*

Wehner   Yes.

Kurten   You were lost.

Wehner   Mmm. (*Pause. Still deep in thought.*)
Tell me
do you think your father loved
your mother?

Kurten (*pause*)   May I ask an earnest question
By way of a reply?

Wehner *remains silent.*

Kurten   Have you ever been in love?

Wehner (*pause*)   I don't believe so, no.

Kurten   How, then, would you define love?

Wehner (*thinks*)   Selflessness. Trust. Understanding.
Affection. Happiness –

Kurten   And how have you arrived at this definition?
From books, from art?
From the dictionary?

Wehner   From observation.

Kurten   Observing who?

Wehner   People.

Kurten   Strangers?

Wehner   Yes. No. The people around me.

Kurten   Your family?

Wehner   Yes.

Kurten   Your parents?

Wehner   Naturally.

Kurten   Did your parents love each other?

Wehner   Yes.

Kurten   How do you know?

Wehner   I just know.

Kurten   But how?

Wehner   They must have.

Kurten   They must have?
Because daddy must love mummy?

Wehner   How does this answer my question?

Kurten (*pause*)   I don't suppose it does.

Wehner   Because what your parents had doesn't sound
  like love
it sounds more like
brutality.

Kurten   Brutality belongs to love.

Wehner   I don't believe that.

They stare defiantly at each other.

Tell me more about your childhood.

Kurten   When I was eight I ran away from home for the
first time

I thought myself quite the grown-up.
That was when I killed my first two.

Wehner (*visibly shaken by this*)   You haven't mentioned this
before.

Kurten   Oh it was a fumbling, silly affair.
I was playing with two boys my own age on the banks of
the Rhine
Their parents were picnicking nearby
We had found a makeshift raft, and one of the boys and
myself floated out on it, not far
I thought it might be funny to push him into the water, so
I did. He got trapped under the raft and I found that, by
shifting my weight, I could thwart his attempts to draw
breath.

He cannot help but smile.

I shouldn't laugh I know.
The other one dived in to save him but the little fool
couldn't swim.
They both drowned.

I hid in a nearby bush for nigh on an hour waiting for
their parents to discover them
And what a commotion they made trying to fish them out!

Wehner (*long pause*)   And how did you feel
Afterwards?

Kurten (*thinks*)   Like I had found a diamond
washed up on the beach.
You still think I am insane?

Wehner   Now I know that you are.

Kurten   Just like you know that daddy loves mummy.

Wehner   If you were sane, there would be horror in you
Horror at what you've done.

Kurten   Horror.
What do you know of horror?
So little that it still causes your head to tighten and your

scrotum to contract
Well, let me tell you about horror, Dr Wehner.

There were many dogs loose in the streets where I grew up
And in the house in which my
family lived,
in the room directly beneath ours,
there lived a man whose job it was to round up these curs
No one ever spoke of the sounds that came from that
  room
But night after night I would lie awake, listening to those
sorry whines and yelps
And yearning to know what went on there.

One evening I was passing the dog-catcher's door
when I noticed it was standing just slightly ajar.
A sweet smell hung about it, and a noise came from within
like the whistle of air from a punctured balloon.
I summoned the courage to peer inside.

It was a charnel house, Dr Wehner,
And through the black cloud of flies
at the far end of the room and standing on newspaper
was the catcher at his killing slab
A small dog trembled upon it.

Just then, I slipped in something and he heard the noise
and turned and saw me there.
I was about to run but then he
smiled,
put his finger to his lips
sssshhh
and beckoned me to come closer.
And I went to him.
I closed the door behind me and I went to him.

He taught me many things that man, many things
He took such pleasure in my happiness
We became great friends and I would visit him regularly
after school.

It was during this time that I made an astonishing

discovery;
that the spilling of blood
its coppery smell, its deep colour,
caused a pleasing sensation in my crotch.
I became quite addicted to that sensation.
You can understand that at least, eh, Dr Wehner?

But, you see, fear is really the dullest side of horror's coin
There comes a point when all that is left to do is to go to it
To close the door behind you and to go to it.

It was a sad day for me when my family left Mulheim for
Dusseldorf.
I wonder what became of my dog-catcher friend?

Wehner   Perhaps a dog tore out his throat.

Kurten   Shame, Dr Wehner.
Shame on you.

A long pause.

Wehner   You first went to prison when you were sixteen,
for theft.
How did you feel about that?

Kurten   Humiliated initially.
Isn't that the purpose of prison?
But humiliation gave way to pride, and the more that they
attempted to erode my dignity, the more determined I
became that I would have my revenge.

Wehner   Is that why you murdered, for revenge?

Kurten   My young friend
All told I have spent twenty-seven years of my life in
prison.
Twenty-seven years.
And never for more than petty theft.
I was unjustly persecuted
So if I then went on to unjustly persecute others, it is the
State that is directly responsible.

Wehner   Well I'd be the last to champion the prison system
but that hardly explains the drowning of those two boys.

Kurten   Then what does?

Wehner   I don't know
Perhaps you despised their innocence
An innocence that you were denied.

Kurten   Innocence?
I've had a mother and her daughter take turns at sucking my prick
Now tell me that doesn't cause even a slight 'frisson' in your liberal loins.

Wehner   It disgusts me, that's all.

Kurten   You little hypocrite!
Trying to keep your precious world in order!
Do you know what I was doing in my teens
When you were getting all confused at the sight of your mother's bloomers?!
I was fucking dogs and sheep and pigs whilst sticking them
    with knives
Pigs were the best, you know why?
The noises they made –

And **Kurten** *suddenly begins to squeal like a pig at* **Wehner**.
Wehner *bolts out of his seat, terrified. The squeals grow louder and
then the lights just cut out.*

VIII: Darkness

Wehner   GUARD!!!

The entire theatre has been plunged into darkness. **Wehner** *stumbles
around in panic, calling for the guard, and then there is complete
silence. Finally, from within the blackness comes* **Kurten**'s *calm
tones.*

Kurten   Never there when you need them these guards
always sloping off for a sly cigarette.

Wehner   What's going on?!

Kurten   Power failure
Happens all the time down here.
You're not scared of the dark, are you, Dr Wehner?

Wehner   Just stay where you are, Mr Kurten.

Kurten   The dark has always been good to me.
There's nothing I liked better than a spell in solitary
confinement.
What do you think of in the dark, Dr Wehner?
Naked women perhaps; their skin against yours, their hair
brushing your belly, is that it?
Not me. I would sit there in the blackness and dream of
open wounds and carnage, of exploding bridges and
poisoning reservoirs and feeding sharp sweets to children –

Wehner   GUARD!!

Kurten   What a story for your future children, Wehner.
How they'll thrill when you tell them:
Trapped in the dark with the Dusseldorf Ripper.

The lights snap back on. **Kurten** *stands only inches away from*
Wehner.

And you lived to tell the tale!

The stare into each other's eyes.

Wehner   The man that stands before you today is a
monster.

IX: Wehner rehearses his opening speech

Lights change. **Wehner** *half-addresses the audience jury style.*

Wehner   I make no more attempt to deny that than he
would himself.

He stands accused of nine murders proper, seven
attempted.

By his own admission, he is guilty of over forty counts of
arson.
He killed men, women, children, animals, killed anything
he found.
This man is a monster.

So I do not ask you to have mercy on this man, this
monster, how could I?
But
This man was once a child
Spare a thought for him
Spare a thought for the child that Peter Kurten once was.

Guilt is not the question here, sanity is
And Section 51 defines *in*sanity as 'a state of consciousness
or a diseased disturbance of mental activity which impedes
the operation of free will'.
So
This would seem to be our dilemma;
Does Peter Kurten suffer from such a disturbance that
might absolve him of responsibility for his crimes?

But I believe this to be a case that will test the very
parameters of our definitions
For it is not just Peter Kurten that stands trial here
But society itself.

(*Pleased with himself.*) Yes.

A society, members of the jury, where children can be
abused in the most horrific of ways, with no ear to hear
their screams.
A society that locks away its failures with no counsel, no
guidance, merely the reaffirmation of violence as the final
solution. A society, members of the jury, with no foresight.
And a society with no foresight
Has no future.

That Kurten should be taken from society is beyond debate
But do we punish murder with murder?
Become what we condemn?
Or do we strive to understand?
To prevent rather than cure?

Do we try to turn an evil mind to one of decency and
good?
It's a simple question;
Do we bear monsters?
Or do we create them?

Kurten *shuffles past* **Wehner** *and sits down. He seems heavy,
sad. He produces a rag from his pocket and begins to clean his shoes.*
Wehner *watches.*

Wehner   Or do we create them?

X: A glimpse

Kurten *stops and looks up at* **Wehner**.

Kurten   Forgive me.

Wehner *looks puzzled.*

Kurten   For my behaviour yesterday
I've not been feeling myself lately
I didn't mean to
offend you.

Wehner   It's not my job to be

He hiccoughs.

offended.

Kurten (*smiles*)   You have wind.

Wehner   In the legal profession it seems to be obligatory
to

He hiccoughs.

drink after lunch-time. I haven't

And again.

the belly for it.

Kurten   Listen to me
When you next feel about to hiccough, tell me first.

Wehner *looks bemused but decides to go along with it anyway. A long pause.*

Wehner *(hiccoughs)*   Now.

They both laugh.

Kurten   Again. Concentrate.

Wehner *does. A very long pause.*

Wehner   Now.

Nothing happens. Long pause. He's not going to hiccough.

It's gone.

Kurten *smiles faintly, sadly. He goes back to polishing his shoes and then stops.*

Kurten   These shoes have lost their shine.
I used to be able to see myself in them
Now all I see is dull leather.
I can't go to trial in these.

Wehner *(pause)*   We'll find you some good shoes.

They regard each other. Something passes between them.

What happened after you were released from prison?

Kurten   I went home
My mother had left
I set a barn alight.

Wehner   Why?

Kurten   So I could watch the people try to put it out
Their distress aroused me
And the flames were very beautiful
I never went home again.

From 1900 to 1904, I was in prison again.
On release I was called up for service but I deserted
Monster I may be
Idiot I am not.

I set more fires, I continued to steal. From 1905 to 1912, I

think, I was in prison
Yes, Munster Prison
That was actually quite an amusing time. I was given a job
in the prison hospital and managed to poison several of the
inmates.

Which brings me to Christine Klein.

XI: Christine is woken

Music. During the next speech, the mannequin begins to stir under the sheet.

Wehner   Christine Klein spent only thirteen summers on
this earth
She was Kurten's first recorded victim.
I visited the Klein family as part of my research for the
case
You wouldn't have known they were only in their forties
I didn't tell them I was representing their daughter's
murderer
They welcomed me in.

The mannequin begins to sit up. The sheet slips from its face.

It was early morning and three places were set for
breakfast.
Whilst they recounted the events of eighteen years previous
they ate
It surprised me that they could eat
I kept glancing at that empty place at the table.

The mannequin starts its walk to centre stage. It carries with it a grotesque doll, clothed in a wedding dress.

On the

Kurten   twenty-fifth of May 1913

Wehner   someone had broken into their house by night

Kurten   intending only to rob them but instead I

Wehner   crept into their daughter's bedroom

Kurten   where a black, black urge came upon me. I

Wehner   strangled her

Kurten   put my fingers up her

Wehner   and cut

Kurten   her throat. It happened silently.

Wehner   They slept through the whole thing.

Kurten   It took me three minutes.

Wehner   They didn't have any other children
Did they have a lodger?
Who was that extra place for?

The mannequin kneels centre stage. She combs the doll's hair.

Kurten   The funny thing was I dropped my handkerchief

Wehner   in her bedroom. The police found it the next
day

Kurten   and it had my initials on it

Wehner   P.K.

Kurten   But by a stroke of luck

Wehner   Tragically

Kurten   the girl's uncle's name was Peter *Klein*.

Wehner   He was tried for Christine's murder

Kurten   They acquitted him anyway, for lack of evidence,
but

Wehner   neither was he cleared, and he died with that
stigma around him.

Kurten   I truly believed that God was on my side

Wehner   I couldn't take my eyes off that bowl and its
now cold contents.
I wondered if perhaps they'd set the place for *me*.

They said they were glad that the real killer had been caught.

Kurten   The next day I sat in the café opposite the Klein house.

Wehner   They said they hoped that he would be executed

Kurten   reading about the murder in the morning paper.

Wehner   They said that most of his victims were still alive

Kurten   everybody in the café was talking about it

Wehner   but that nobody wanted to hear about them, only him.

Kurten   All this amount of horror and indignation did me good.

Wehner   What about the victims, what was it like for them

Kurten   and to be sitting there

Wehner   knowing

Kurten   knowing

Wehner   knowing

Kurten   knowing

Wehner   that the man who had done it

Kurten   that I had done it

Wehner   was living, breathing, smiling, laughing.

Kurten   I had killed her.

Wehner   What about them? What about the victims?

Kurten   And nobody

Wehner   Didn't they matter?!

Kurten   Nobody knew.

The mannequin / Christine lets a shower of red confetti fall across the doll that she holds. All is silent. **Wehner** *walks to her and wrests the doll from her hands. He gently pulls her up to stand.*

Wehner   I said to them that people were bound to be
more interested in Kurten because he had led such a
unique life
whereas his victims had only been unique
in their manner of dying.

He leads Christine back to the place from which she rose. He lays her down and she looks up at him plaintively. He covers her face with the sheet as before. The doll still lies centre stage.

I wished I hadn't said that.

He picks up the doll and places it on the evidence stand.

All I could see was that bowl, that spoon, that saucer, that
cup
All untouched.

He stares at the doll.

Thirteen summers.

XII: The diamond revealed

Kurten   Have you ever wondered why it is
that a young man like yourself should choose to defend the
guilty?
Choice, you see
that's the heart of it
You choose to believe that I am insane
because you choose not to believe in evil
Yet you know that they are both only terms of convenience
and distant relations of truth
Why do you support the structures you distrust?

Wehner   Because
without structure
society would collapse.

Kurten   There is no such thing as society.

Wehner   That's
absurd.

Kurten   After killing Christine Klein
I attempted a similar crime only weeks later
but without success
However
I did manage to throttle two young ladies unconscious and
on one occasion
I set about a young couple out strolling, this time
   employing a small hatchet.
I didn't kill them,
merely spoiled their evening,
but the sight of their blood on the cobblestones
led me to a most powerful discharge
and after that —

Wehner   How *do* you feel about your father, Peter?

Kurten   I hated him
Justus.

Wehner   When did you last see him?

Kurten   Many years ago. I forget.

Wehner   Let me remind you.
You saw him in the spring of last year.
He had fallen ill and he called for you. You went to him.
You nursed him. You gave him money, clothes, food.

Kurten *remains silent.*

Wehner   The Berlin Alexanderplatz found him yesterday.
He didn't deny that your childhood had been
troubled
but he also recalled many happy times you and he had
spent together.
Your visits to the beach near Hamburg for instance.

He used to tell you a story, do you remember?
You never tired of hearing it.

About how a ship had gone down off that coast, decades
before.

No one had survived and its cargo of treasure had been
    lost
But he also told you how
on stormy nights
that ship could still be glimpsed in the distance, between
the peaks of the crashing waves, its wounded hull, its
splintered mast, and how rumour had it that were you to
comb through the shells and the pebbles, on the morning
after such a ghostly sighting

Kurten   You would find a diamond

Wehner   A diamond from that long-lost cargo

Kurten   Washed up on the beach.

Wehner   How *do* you feel, Peter, about the man who
beat you, the man who raped your sisters and your
mother?!

Kurten (*angry*)   In 1913 I was imprisoned again
In 1921, I went to Altenberg.

The mannequin sits up. Its mask has gone. It is now **Frau
Kurten**. *She hisses.*

Frau Kurten   Peter

Kurten   And it was there that

Frau Kurten   What

Kurten   I met

Frau Kurten   have

Kurten   the woman

Frau Kurten   you

Kurten   that was to be

Frau Kurten   done?!

Kurten   my wife.

Kurten *exits*. **Wehner** *turns surprised to face* **Frau Kurten**.

XIII: First meeting with Frau Kurten

Wehner   Frau Kurten.
It's good of you to see me.
This must be
upsetting for you.

She remains completely impassive, her gaze fixed upon **Wehner**. *He feels very foolish, very awkward.*

I mean this must be
very
upsetting for you
You've uh
You've spoken to your husband?

Frau Kurten   I think he would rather have seen a priest.

Wehner   I didn't know he was a religious man.

Frau Kurten   I didn't say that he was
but I expect he is a fearful one, and they do say that all
fear is the fear of God.

Wehner (*long pause*)   Do they? (*Long pause.*)
Please, take a seat.

After a moment's hesitation, she does so.

Frau Kurten   Will they kill my husband, Dr Wehner?

Wehner (*pause*)   At first, I thought not
But these are uncertain days and the people are angry
It's the blood of our leaders they want
It's the blood of your husband they may well get.

Frau Kurten *bows her head.*

Wehner   But I will do my best for him. You must help
me in this.

You must be very candid about your relationship with
Peter.

She nods faintly. This is difficult for her.

Frau Kurten   Before Peter, my life was
a shameful, aimless one
I was a
working girl
for a time.

Wehner (*pause*)   You were a prostitute.

Frau Kurten   Does that surprise you?

Wehner   No.
I mean
yes.
But no.
Please
continue.

Frau Kurten   Some of the men
the regulars anyway
had genuine care for me.
I know they did.
In fact, it was one of my regulars that convinced me to
leave the trade.
He was a gardener by profession and I was his mistress for
eight years.
You see his wife was poorly and he thought it cruel to
divorce her so we waited for her to die but when she did
he refused to marry me so
So I shot him, Dr Wehner.
I took a gun and I shot the man I loved.
I served four years for it.
But that was nothing compared to the sentence I imposed
upon myself.
And then I met Peter.
It was ten years ago in Altenberg.
(*Smiles.*) He was obviously a man well-versed in the art of
attracting women. I had met a million like him.
Or so I thought.

XIV: The art of seduction

Wehner (*to audience*)   The art of seduction, Peter said, was much akin to that of murder!

Music. The next scene is in the style of an old slapstick silent movie, complete with jerky movements and flickering lights. **Kurten** *re-enters.*

Wehner   First, visualise your goal!

Kurten *looks at* **Frau Kurten**, *then at the audience. He rubs his hands together greedily. He presents* **Frau Kurten** *with a flower, which she refuses.* **Kurten** *ponders another approach.*

Wehner   Different people respond to different things.

Kurten *then presents her with a parcel. She refuses.*

Wehner   Be persistent!

Kurten *offers her the gift again. She hesitates, then accepts.*

Wehner   At last a result!

Kurten *rubs his hands together and attempts to kiss her but she runs away, leaving him standing there, lips puckered.*

Wehner   Oh-oh! You must be prepared to look a fool!

Frau Kurten *stands downstage, blushing coquettishly. With a sigh,* **Kurten** *begins to chase her playfully around the room. At some point he stops and looks at the audience with an expression of exasperation.*

Wehner   Patience is required!

Kurten *recommences the chase and finally catches her.*

Wehner   When you are close enough to take advantage, do not!

Kurten *drops to bended knee before her.*

Wehner   Convince her that your intentions are honourable!

Kurten *mouths this statement. She turns away from him.*

Wehner   Of course some people need more convincing than others!

Kurten *presents her with a ring. She is flattered but still refuses.*

Wehner   And even so, there are some who just aren't looking for honour!

Kurten *paces angrily. He is confused. And then it comes to him.*

Wehner   Finally, the proper approach will present itself to you!

Kurten *smiles evilly and produces the scissors. Keeping them behind his back he advances on* **Frau Kurten**. *She refuses him again so he presents them to her. She is immediately more conducive. He makes stabbing gestures.*

Wehner   The most direct approach is often the right one!

She swoons and embraces him. She proffers her hand and he slips the ring onto her finger.

Wehner   From that moment on, it's simply a matter of time!

They sigh blissfully. Music ends.

XV: To love is to need

Wehner   He threatened to kill you?
He forced you to marry him?

Frau Kurten   No, Dr Wehner.
I chose to marry him.

Wehner   I don't understand this, not at all.

Frau Kurten   To love is to need.
Needs are unfathomable things.
He needed me, for whatever reasons
and from that moment on,
I needed him.

Wehner   And do you still?

Frau Kurten I don't want to die alone.
And who would have me now?

She faces **Wehner**. *He cannot think of what to say.*

Please
I'm not looking for reassurance
Are you married?

Wehner Me? No.
I went straight from school to studying law
It's paid dividends professionally but it's left me little time for
anything else.

Frau Kurten But you wanted this?

Wehner Of course!
My parents were highly principled, you see.
The only way to change a system is from within.
There were times when I wished my life had not been
quite so taken up with academia but on the whole I feel
it's been to my . . .

Frau Kurten Advantage?

Wehner (*pause*) Yes.
I want to understand, Frau Kurten.

Frau Kurten Perhaps it's better that you don't.
You seem a decent man.
These are dangerous days for decent men.

It wasn't much of a marriage we had, I suppose,
but for the first few years it was stable at least.
He worked as a moulder in Altenberg and became an
active Union member, always home promptly from work
and content to stay home.
Yes.
We were content.
But in 1925, he was made redundant, and that was when
things began to change.

Wehner Change?

XVI: The death of passion

Lighting change on **Wehner**'*s last word.*

Kurten   How beautiful she is.

Frau Kurten   Yes, change.

Kurten   How noble in her sadness.

Frau Kurten   How does one describe

Kurten   A beacon of hurt

Frau Kurten   The death of passion

Kurten   Shining for miles

Frau Kurten   to one who's hardly lived?
You touch and yet you do not touch

Kurten   I tried. I tried
to make it work

Frau Kurten   You speak and yet you are not heard

Kurten   I tried to swallow down the urge

Frau Kurten   You learn to weep without a sound

Kurten   With the morning coffee and the goodbye kiss

Frau Kurten   You look for meanings in the tiniest things

Kurten   Not that it was ever a matter of lust

Frau Kurten   You peck at the ground for the crumbs of
affection

Kurten   I respected her far too much for that

Frau Kurten   You try to sleep back to back

Kurten   But when I did venture between her thighs

Frau Kurten   You count the notches on his spine

Kurten   I thought of killing to keep me hard

Frau Kurten   Your eyes staring into the dark

Kurten Of little Christine's final contractions

Frau Kurten Your hopes dying at your lips

Kurten Of little Christine's startled eyes

Frau Kurten The passion fades. But the need survives.

Kurten How beautiful she was.

Frau Kurten Yes, change.

Lighting change.

And that was when he returned to Dusseldorf.

She exits.

XVII: Birth

Kurten Yes Back!
And the sky was a bloody red
Just as it had been for Jack
in London 1888!
Oh yes!
I had read of him avidly
(in prison no less)
and I had thought;
now there's a man after my own heart!
And what with the clouds on fire, it was as if Jack himself
was saying
'Peter!
You are one of us now
One of an elite
Destined to take your place in the Chambers of Horrors
and the nightmares of children for all time!'
And as I walked through those familiar streets
I chanced upon the scene of an accident involving a horse
And I stood amongst the crowd that had gathered round
and I came in my pants.
I felt like a king! No more denial, no more pretending

like those 'innocent' bystanders!
A thousand moments came together, I understood
my true nature
The Dusseldorf Ripper
is born.

XVIII: Second letter home

Lights slowly upon **Wehner**.

Wehner   Dusseldorf, April 1931
Dear Mama
Dear Papa
Will you be coming to Dusseldorf?
I need to talk to you.
Perhaps it's just the pressure to prove oneself but
I feel myself
floundering in this case.
I am not sleeping well, and as a result I am not
thinking clearly I
can't seem to remember what
   brought me to this point
It's as if my thoughts are not my own,
never were.

Do you know where Eva is? She was the only girl I ever
kissed
I was eleven years old. It was one summer, behind the
rosebush. I might have kissed her again
but you called me back to my books.
She thought me a little coward.

Please write to me.
I cannot confide in my colleagues.
Your loving son
Justus.

Kurten *appears behind him and the way that* **Wehner** *reacts to
him* **Kurten** *may as well be just a voice in his head.*

Kurten   She spoke very highly of you.

Wehner   Who did?

Kurten   My wife. I wouldn't blame you at all.

Wehner   For what?

Kurten   Don't you think she's an attractive woman?

Wehner   I don't see what that's —

Kurten   Yes. I can tell that you do.
Sunday afternoons at the Rhine Meadows, the women used
to flock around me. I could count them ten to each hand.
I know these things. I know people.
And I know her.

Wehner   What are you suggesting?

Kurten   It's as I told you; the direct approach, especially
with her. She was a whore after all. You'd only have to
touch her and she'd surrender to your every whim. And a
woman in such a position, listen now; she'd be grateful
enough to be discreet.

Wehner   Are you implying that I might . . .

Kurten   It's only natural. You both have years of desire
pent up inside you. What harm could there be in it?

Wehner   It would be completely unethical!

Kurten   Lust has no ethics.

Wehner   I can assure you, Mr Kurten — no, I'm not even
going to assure you, the whole idea is preposterous!
Preposterous!
And impossible.

Kurten   Please. You misunderstand me. I am not
accusing you. Why, I share her high opinion of you.

Wehner   You're my client. She's your wife.

Kurten   Yes. And what good am I to her now?
I just want her to be happy. To have what she wants.

Wehner   And what is that?

Kurten   She needs a man who can bring some
decency into her life. Some
purity.
All the things that I could never give her.

Wehner   Well, it's academic, Peter.
Even if I wanted to, I couldn't.
You do care about her. It's obvious.
She'll be all right.

Kurten   The wife of the Dusseldorf Ripper?
Think about it, Justus; if not you, then who? Who will see
beyond it?

*A long pause. Subtly the lights have changed, and they are now back
in the prison cell.*

You see this wasp?

Kurten *is kneeling on the cell floor, looking at the dying insect.*
Wehner *joins him.*

Wehner   How did that get in here?

Kurten   It circled round my head for a time, and then it
spiralled to the ground. It's hardly moved for over an hour.
I've been watching it die.

Wehner   Why, Peter? Malice?
Or sympathy?

Kurten   You know
I can't tell any more.

And for some time they kneel there watching it die.

Wehner   You returned to Dusseldorf in 1925.
What happened between then and 1929?

Kurten   I watched. I waited. I set a few fires here and
there.
I cultivated the image of a gentle and pleasant man.
And then it began.

XIX: The reign of terror

Wehner February 3rd 1929

Kurten *carries his scissors as one might an umbrella, over his shoulder.*

Kurten I went out walking in the mood for love.

Wehner One Frau Kuhn, a servant girl

Kurten Someone's last full moon above

Wehner Twenty-four stab wounds to the body and head

Kurten I broke off the point of my brand new scissors

And on this line, **Kurten** *begins to tap his foot to the rhythm of the words.*

Wehner She crawled to the hospital two streets away

Kurten No one takes a pride in their work any more

Wehner They saved her life but she'd lost her memory

Kurten I ground them down to a point once more.

By now, **Kurten** *is moving his whole body in time to the words and smiling wickedly.* **Wehner** *watches him in horror and anger, but almost imperceptibly he too is beginning to tap his foot.*

Wehner February 13th, Rudolf Scheer

Kurten A drunken old man reeling through the streets

Wehner Stabbed twenty times in the body and head

Kurten Still, at least he died during carnival week!

Kurten *shuffles towards* **Wehner**, *sending up the whole thing.*

Wehner March 9th, little Rose Ohliger

Kurten Eight years old and eyes like the night

Kurten *has taken* **Wehner***'s arm and now they pivot around each other.*

Wehner Stabbed thirteen times in the body and head

Kurten } But I didn't tamper with her 'til after she was dead
Wehner } But he didn't tamper with her 'til after she was dead

Wehner *is aghast with himself for joining in.*

Wehner   Her body found dumped on a building site

Kurten   It was my tender heartedness

Wehner   He stood amongst the crowd that watched them carry her away

Kurten   I would never torture children.

Kurten *continues to dance round* **Wehner**.

Wehner   April 29th, two failed attacks

Kurten   But an illiterate named Strausberg was committed for that.

Wehner   July 30th, Emma Gross found strangled

Kurten   But that was a work of (*Thinks.*) copy-cattery

Kurten *has grabbed* **Wehner**'s *shoulders and they are rising up and dropping down alternately.* **Wehner** *allows him to do this. He cannot help but smile.*

Wehner   At least it secured the release of Strausberg

Kurten   And still the sincerest form of

Kurten } FLATTERY!!
Wehner }

Wehner *is well and truly embroiled in the dance.*

Wehner   August 21st, young Frau Mantel

Kurten   I stabbed her once as she walked to the fair.

Wehner   And Anna Goldhausen. And Gustav Kornblum.

Kurten   Lucky he was wearing heavy leather braces

Wehner   They all survived, though they each lost blood

Kurten   They were cut right through and his trousers fell down!

The both laugh uproariously. **Kurten** *holds his scissors aloft and they each take hold of separate ends and rotate, changing ends when they change direction.*

Wehner   Saturday August the 23rd

Kurten   I went to a fair at the Flehe suburb

Wehner   Louise was fourteen, Gertrude was five

Kurten   I sent the older to buy some fags

And now **Wehner** *is quite carried away with it.*

Wehner   Whilst she was gone, he took Gertrude's life

Now they are playing a bizarre form of pat-a-cake.

Kurten   Now the Bavarians know how to make a knife

On this last word, **Kurten** *slaps* **Wehner** *on the face.* **Wehner** *stands stunned, horrified at the realisation of what he's been doing.*

Wehner   When Louise returned, he killed her too

Kurten   But not before I got
my

Kurten
Wehner } Change.

XX: Third letter home

But this letter is a scream of rage.

Wehner   Dusseldorf, April 1931
Dear Mama, Dear Papa
It's all so easy, isn't it?!
We say killed. We say dead. We recount the atrocities like we would a shopping list and then we find excuses, causes, loopholes, technicalities. People live and die by slips of the tongue, but we can still laugh about it over a drink and commend ourselves for our cleverness.
And meanwhile little Gertrude's parents, or Christine's or Louise's, are living with loss, by day, by night, setting an extra

place at the table for loss because it is loss that shares their home, loss that shares their beds!

Every one of those victims was someone's daughter, someone's lover, someone's brother, son. Imagine their thoughts. Imagine the details of their thoughts.

Imagine thinking about your child's last moments on this earth, alone, afraid, the child that you made, the child that you saw smile for the first time, that you saw walk, that you heard talk. What noises did it make in that last moment?

What look was in its eyes? Did it feel pain when the blade went in?

Did it call out your name?

Because maybe she walked out the door that night and out of your life and maybe you didn't even say goodbye.

And you sit there sorting through her things, the tatty toys she used to hug, her tiny shoes, her simple books, and you pack them away in boxes with your hopes and dreams, the ornaments of a life, and you think maybe if I had done this or that then maybe she'd still be alive maybe she is still alive maybe there's been some mistake and then it hits you again the deafening slam of the irreversible; she's gone, she's gone for ever

She's gone

for ever.

Is that too sentimental for you, 'Papa'?

Is that too 'emotive' for you, 'Mama'?

Is that too *true* for you? What, are you

ashamed of me?!

Are you *proud* of me?!

Well damn you and your morals!

Left, right, it's all the same.

What's true is that you

USED me, Mama, you

USED me, Papa, and where are you now, now that I need you, what am I to *do*

WHY

DON'T

YOU

WRITE!

Your loving son
Justus.
(*Laughs Scornfully.*) Justice, Justus,

Justice.

XXI: Murder and seduction

Frau Kurten *appears behind* **Wehner**.

Frau Kurten   Justus.
There's a certain irony in that.

Wehner   Irony requires an element of chance.
I don't know your name.

Frau Kurten   Eva. Eva.

Wehner *begins to laugh. It is a strange laugh and he cannot help himself.*

Frau Kurten   What?

Wehner (*the laugh has suddenly died*)   Tell me
Eva
How could you live with him and not know?

Frau Kurten   That he was the Dusseldorf Ripper?

Wehner *remains silent. He realises the redundancy of the question.*

Frau Kurten (*pause*)   I worked in a restaurant every evening.
And every evening, Peter would come to meet me and walk
me home. Every evening. Just in case.

(*She giggles. Then stops.*) He must have been

She looks at **Wehner** *with real horror.*

whilst I was at work?

Wehner *watches her terrified eyes recover their defence.*

Frau Kurten   Besides, I was too busy suspecting him of

adultery.
He didn't even have to make an effort to attract women.
Once he took me to the Meadows and introduced me as his
sister, so I could see how they were with him
and it was
quite astounding
and all of them young and pretty and with such temptation
it's a miracle that he didn't succumb more often
And he was honest about it
mostly
One afternoon I came home and found him in our bed with a
girl.
I made them coffee.

Wehner *looks blankly at her.*

Frau Kurten   What else was I to do?
You'll come to see that such things are of little importance.
He needed me.

Wehner (*long pause*)   But you have your needs too
don't you?

Frau Kurten (*pause*)   Yes. Yes, like anyone.
It's fortunate that I can suppress them.

Wehner   Why?

Frau Kurten (*pause*)   I'm not getting any younger.

Wehner   You're still an attractive women.

Frau Kurten   I'm
I was a whore
I shot the man I loved
Do you understand?
I shot him.

Wehner   So you deny yourself affection.

He draws ever nearer towards her.

Is that it?
Because nothing you can do is ever enough.

Frau Kurten *is tense.*

Frau Kurten   Of course, there were times when Peter's behaviour upset me.
Twice I had to convince girls he had been with

Wehner   Can you help me, Eva?

Frau Kurten   Twice I had to convince them

Wehner   Can you help me understand?

Frau Kurten   not to press charges for rough behaviour

Wehner   But didn't that strike you as

Frau Kurten   Perhaps!
Perhaps it did.
But tell me
Why should I have cared?

Kurten *appears behind* **Wehner**.

Kurten   You only have to touch her, Justus.

Frau Kurten   I think about how kind he was, how caring.

Kurten   She would surrender to your every whim.

Frau Kurten   How we would sit in bed and discuss the day's events.

Kurten   You see how vulnerable she is.

Frau Kurten   Always the perfect gentleman.

Kurten   How she needs your arms around her.

Frau Kurten   And then I have to pinch myself.

Kurten   What harm could there be in it?

Frau Kurten   Remind myself of what he's done.

Kurten   Two lost people finding solace in each other.

Frau Kurten   The shame of it all.

Kurten   Taking comfort from the touch of skin against skin.

Frau Kurten   Can it be true, Dr Wehner?

Kurten   No ugliness. No brutality.

Frau Kurten   Can it be true?

Kurten   Love and only love.

Frau Kurten   Did I marry a monster?

Kurten   What harm could there be in it?

Frau Kurten (*crying now*)   Did I marry a monster??!!

Kurten   You only have to touch her.

Wehner *pulls her to him and kisses her. She resists only for a moment. His hand grasps at her breast. They sink to the ground and the lights fade with them. In the darkness, we hear* **Kurten**'s *laughter.*

XXII: Daydream

Kurten   Another fantasy of mine
at the time of the killings
was that of saving
the city of Dusseldorf
from its dreaded nemesis
the vampire the werewolf the monster the ripper
For I was the only one capable of such a feat
where even the massed ranks of the Dusseldorf police and
the Berlin Alexanderplatz had failed!
I would emerge triumphant from the long and bloody battle
though severely wounded
and the people would be so thankful to me
would so admire me
that they would throw a huge torchlit procession in my
honour.
In fact, so impressed would they be
that they would storm police headquarters and demand
the deposition of the commissioner
and appoint me
in his place

and the name of
Peter Kurten!
Saviour of Dusseldorf!
would be lauded
throughout Germany
and the world!!

Kurten *buries his face in his hands. When he looks up, that brief glimpse of lightness is gone, and his eyes are blank, killer's eyes.*

But that was just a daydream.

XXIII: The reign of terror continues

Lights up on **Wehner** *and* **Frau Kurten**. *During the next scene,* **Wehner** *touches her, examines her as if she is no more than a piece of meat, or a rag doll. Her voice is dead.*

Wehner   August 29th, he killed Maria Hahn

Kurten   I stuffed her vagina with earth and leaves

Frau Kurten   Attempted to crucify her on two nearby trees

Wehner   But the body was too heavy

Kurten   So I hid her in a shallow grave

Frau Kurten   To which he sometimes would return

Wehner   To discharge on the soil.

Kurten   Then one day in September

Frau Kurten   in the space of half an hour

Wehner   Attacked two women and a man

Kurten   I drank blood from his forehead

Frau Kurten   The monster is a vampire too

Wehner   Or so the papers said

Kurten   But all that I was trying to do
was keep my love life fresh.

Frau Kurten   The police now thought this work to be

Wehner   The work of two killers, maybe three

Kurten   So then I got myself a hammer

Frau Kurten   To confuse the police further

Wehner   And sturdier too when taking a life

Kurten   But mainly just to add some spice.

Frau Kurten   Late September

Wehner   Ida Reuter

Kurten   Bashed her head in with my hammer.

Frau Kurten   Ten days later

Wehner   Now October

Kurten   Did the same to Elizabeth Dorrier.

Frau Kurten   October 25th, one Frau Meurer

Wehner   Beaten senseless

Kurten   but not murdered.

Frau Kurten   That same night, one Frau Wanders

Wehner   Dealt her one swift hammer stroke

Kurten   But would you believe it
my hammer broke!

Frau Kurten   Gertrude Albermann was five

Wehner   November 7th, the day she died

Kurten   But I wouldn't use a hammer to kill a child

Frau Kurten   He strangled and stabbed her thirty-six times

Wehner   They found her body in an old factory yard

Kurten   But only because I wrote a letter to the paper

Frau Kurten   telling where to find Gertrude and where to
find another

Wehner   So it was three months later, only then

Kurten   that they found the grave of Maria Hahn.

Lights on **Kurten**. *He addresses the audience.*

Jack would have been proud of the letter.
It showed them up for the idiots they were.
It was my final satisfaction
to know that I had beaten them
for the world to see
my taunting letter in print.
Oh yes.
Jack
would have been proud.

XXIV: Refrain 3

Frau Kurten *looks at* **Wehner**, *and suddenly she comes alive. She reaches out to touch him.*

Frau Kurten   Peter?

Wehner, *horrified, recoils from her touch and staggers away.*

Wehner   Back in May of 1929, a young girl, Maria Budlick, approached a man in the street and asked him if he knew the whereabouts of a hostel. He offered to show her the way. She went with him.

Frau Kurten   Peter, what is it that's happened?

Wehner   When he led her into a park, she became scared. The man was insistent that she should follow him. Just then, to Maria's relief, a second man arrived and offered to escort her from the woods. This was Peter Kurten.

Frau Kurten   The police were looking for you.

Wehner   He took her to his home, fed her, then told her he would take her to the hostel. They went via the Grafenberger woods, where he attempted to strangle her.

Frau Kurten   What have you done this time?

Wehner   Suddenly, a change of heart came upon him. He asked her if she remembered where his house was. She said no, and he let her go. She didn't tell the police but months later mentioned the incident in a letter to a friend. The letter was misdirected.

Frau Kurten   Is it serious?

Wehner   The receiver opened the letter and realising the significance of the incident, informed the authorities who in turn contacted Miss Budlick. She led them to 71 Mettmannerstrasse, Kurten's home.

Frau Kurten   Peter, what is it that's happened?

Wehner   Kurten saw them arrive and fled. He stayed away for two days before contacting his wife. He arranged to meet her the following day in the Hofgarten. They would have a meal and he would explain everything. It was Friday, the 23rd of May, 1930.

Frau Kurten *is right by his ear now.* **Wehner** *squeezes shut his eyes. Her hand touches his shoulder and it is as if* **Wehner** *is being touched by death itself.*

Frau Kurten   Peter, what have you
done?

XXV: Destruction

Kurten   Yes. What *have* you done?

Wehner   What you wanted. What she wanted. What I wanted.
Forsaken everything that I held dear.

Kurten   You mean you fucked my wife.

Wehner   It was a
beautiful
thing.

Kurten   And a brutal thing too, no?

Do you love her?

Wehner   I suppose I must.

Kurten   Then you can't stop there.
You must see it through.

Wehner   What do you mean?

Kurten   When I met Maria that morning and confessed to her who I was,
her first suggestion was that we both kill ourselves.
But I pointed out that there was a large reward for my capture and, were she to turn me in, it would be hers.
The thought mortified her at first, but I convinced her that it would not constitute a betrayal.
I arranged to meet her at Saint Rochus church the next day.
I made sure I was smart for the occasion.
When I arrived, the police were waiting.

Wehner   And so?

Kurten   She didn't turn me in for the reward.
It was an act of love.
She understood what it was that I wanted, needed.
It could not be by my own hand.
For it was the same thing that she wants and needs.

Wehner   And what *is* that???!

Kurten   Destruction, Justus.
Destruction.

Wehner (*exhausted and near to tears*)   But you're *insane*.

Kurten   No. But you know that, don't you?

Wehner   Sane people don't want destruction. Sane people don't murder.

Kurten   Give her what she wants, Justus.

He offers **Wehner** *a hammer. It is a surreal and hideous-looking weapon.* **Wehner** *looks in horror from the hammer to* **Frau Kurten** *and back.*

It's all so easy, isn't it?
We say killed.
We say dead.
We say love.
We say murder.
You have to understand it, Justus.
You have to go to it.

Wehner *still will not take the hammer.*

Kurten   Do you want me to set the scene?
We're in the Grafenberger woods.

Lighting change. The three are bathed in moonlight. **Frau Kurten**
stares up into the light. The set becomes a tangled and sharp network of
trees.

She adores you. She trusts you.
She senses that you can give her what she needs
The annihilation of the self.
She stares out into the night and sings.

Frau Kurten *sings the first few lines of a song appropriate to the*
period.

Kurten   You say: 'What a heavenly voice you have.'

And, though **Kurten** *speaks the words,* **Wehner***'s lips move.*

Frau Kurten   How nice of you to say so. Shall I continue?

Kurten   You say: 'Please'
and you think of her shocking red blood
and how it will look in the moonlight

Frau Kurten *continues to sing.*

Kurten   She says:

Frau Kurten   I'm afraid I don't know any more of the song.

Kurten   You say: 'I'd be happy just listening to those few
lines over and over
It puts me in mind of my mother somehow.'

Wehner *is mesmerised.* **Kurten** *offers the hammer again and, almost* *without thinking* **Wehner** *takes it.*

Frau Kurten *continues to sing.*

Her song fades to a hum. **Wehner** *raises the hammer. It looks as if he is about to strike but he falters.*

Wehner   I can't. I can't. I'm not a murderer. I'm not insane.

Kurten   No. I know.
Go on.

Wehner   I can't, Peter. I love her.

Kurten   You don't love her!
Any more than she loves YOU, you little fool!
Why do you think she let you have her?
She did it for me! It was what I wanted.
She did it because she loves *me*!

Wehner   That's a lie!

Kurten   She says:

Frau Kurten   No, it's true. It's Peter I love. It's Peter I need.

Wehner   Eva.

Kurten   She thought you were a little coward.

Wehner   No.

Kurten   A little mummy's boy.

Wehner   No.

Kurten   She used you, and then she threw you aside.

Wehner   No!

Kurten   Just like dear mama.

Wehner   *No!*

Kurten   Just like dear papa!

Wehner   *NO!!!!*

Wehner *brings the hammer down on* **Frau Kurten**'*s head. We hear the sound of dogs barking.*

XXVI: The art of murder

There follows a long murder sequence. It is quite relentless. **Kurten** *never actually gets involved, but simply directs* **Wehner** *in the act.*
Frau Kurten *totters around for a while. Her fingers touch her head, and it is only when she sees the blood that she realises what has happened and falls.* **Wehner** *strikes her again. She lies still.* **Wehner** *stares at his handiwork with a mixture of horror and exhilaration.*
And then, suddenly, **Frau Kurten** *escapes, invading the audience space.* **Wehner** *bolts after her, catches her and drags her kicking and screaming back to the stage. He strikes her again.* **Kurten** *indicates that* **Wehner** *should strangle her. He does this and she falls limp.* **Wehner** *backs away and she suddenly sits up, coughing and spluttering.* **Wehner** *strangles her again. She collapses. He backs off. She starts to crawl away.* **Wehner** *grabs her and* **Kurten** *directs him to break her legs, which he does.* **Wehner** *stares at the hammer in the moonlight.* **Frau Kurten**, *meanwhile has crawled away again.* **Kurten** *sends* **Wehner** *after her. Slowly he stalks her and strikes her again. He drops the hammer and drags her dead weight back to* **Kurten**. **Wehner** *is exhausted.*

Kurten *sends him back to retrieve the hammer, and in his absence,* **Frau Kurten** *comes round again. Wearily,* **Wehner** *walks to her and strikes her again and again and again.* **Wehner** *is like an animal, beating her head. He screams, a terrible, triumphant scream.* **Frau Kurten** *dies.* **Wehner** *collapses over her body.*

Kurten *straightens his tie, brushes down his suit, as though nothing has happened and ascends the rostra.*

XXVII: Verdict

Kurten   Members of the Jury
You know what this man has done
For myself, I am done with such debates
You will choose your own truth depending on the foundations
you have built your lives upon
And will continue to build upon in the future.
He is insane.
He is insane.

And if you should find different
then God help us all.

Wehner *looks to the audience. He seems quite deranged.*

Wehner Stop it! Stop it!
I am not on trial here!
I AM NOT ON TRIAL!!!

A long pause.

(Bleakly.) The case ended on April the 23rd, 1931
The jury retired for an hour and a half.
Peter was sentenced to death nine times.
The judge said that Peter's crimes were committed in cold
blood and that
throughout the trial
he had created the impression of cleverness, calmness
and considered deliberation.
Peter Kurten, he said,
is normal.

XXVIII: After the verdict

The stage is bathed in red light. **Frau Kurten** *stands. When the lights
come up,* **Wehner** *looks around for the corpse. He looks up at* **Frau
Kurten***, and begins silently to weep.*

Frau Kurten May I see him now?

Weakly, **Wehner** *nods.*

I tried to warn you, Justus.
He
needed me.
In its own way it was
a beautiful thing it –

Wehner *raises his hand 'stop'.* **Frau Kurten** *climbs the steps to her
husband. They stand facing each other. Music reprise of love theme from
Scene XI.*

Wehner   Dusseldorf June 1931
Dear Mama
Dear Papa
I've just learned that the appeal has failed
This is just to say that I won't be requiring you to write to me
any more
I have a new father now.
By the way, I found out about Eva.
She is dead.
Think of me as the same.
Justus.

Lights fade on him. Our focus switches to **Kurten** *and* **Frau
Kurten**. *They stare at each other their eyes speak volumes, of regret,
sadness, love.*

Frau Kurten   Oh Peter
What have you done?

Music ends.

XXIX: Two dying men in a room

Kurten   Justus. I feared you wouldn't come. I wanted to
thank you.

Wehner   What for?

A pause. **Kurten** *smiles fondly.*

Kurten   I had to be sure. I couldn't take the risk. Do you
understand?

A pause.

Wehner   Have you eaten?

Kurten   I have, I have.
Wiener Schnitzel, potatoes, even wine. Excellent.
And do you know, they even allowed me a second portion.

Wehner   Twelve hours until you die, Peter.

How do you feel?

Kurten (*thinks*) Quite full.
Yet I do feel some sadness that I will not live
to hear the children sing about me in the playgrounds,
as they sing about Jack in London.
That is my one regret.

Wehner It will never happen.

Kurten You've regained that old certainty of yours, then.

Wehner Oh no. You did too good a job for that.
A dying man's last spit in the face of life.
But that's all we are; two dead men in a room
What do we matter to children?

A long pause.

Kurten Justus?

Wehner Yes?

Kurten Since the verdict my
dreams have been peaceful, so very
peaceful.

Wehner *says nothing.*

Kurten Is that
how it is for them
out there?

Wehner Some of them, yes.

Kurten And they love each other
without fear, without pain?

Wehner (*pause*) Yes.

Kurten But is that the *truth*?
How do you *know*?

Wehner (*sighs*) I don't, Peter. I don't.
But that's *my* truth.
For now.

Kurten (*pause*) Then why so grim, Justus?

A long pause.

Wehner You've had a lot of mail.

Kurten Hate mail?

Wehner Mostly.

Kurten And the rest?

Wehner (*pause*) Some requesting your autograph.
Some proposing marriage.

Kurten *is quietly pleased.*

Kurten And I hear that Mr Lang intends to make a moving
picture based upon my life. What do you think of that?

Wehner *remains silent.*

Kurten I am not the only, Justus, nor will I be the last.
Even as we speak they are being created, assembled; in the
homes, in the prisons.
In the playgrounds.
And they are, all of them, normal men.

A long pause.

Wehner I'm to ask you if you have a final wish.

Kurten A final wish.
Tell me
how do I look?

Wehner You look fine.

Kurten Honestly?

Wehner Honestly.

Kurten Yes, I have a final wish.

He extends his hand. **Wehner** *looks at it, then takes it. They grip each
other tightly.* **Wehner** *touches his head against* **Kurten**'s *hand and*
Kurten *tightens his grip further causing* **Wehner** *considerable pain.*
Wehner *squirms and* **Kurten** *moves close to his lips.*

It is that I should live just long enough
to hear my own blood gushing from my neck.

Kurten *relinquishes his grip but* **Wehner** *still holds onto it.* **Kurten** *has to extricate his hand.* **Kurten** *assumes his position as in Scene 1.*

XXX: Execution/1952

Wehner   And as I stood there in that arcade, amongst the
laughing children
I saw that finally
as he said he would
he had what he had wanted.
I heard once more the ringing of the poor sinner's bell across
the years

Kurten *repeats his actions, scissors in hand, as in Scene I. The swan rises and* **Frau Kurten** *stands watching her husband walk to his death.*

Wehner   and I could only watch him
the ripper the monster
the legend
watch him mount the guillotine steps
watch them raise their blade of polished steel and remember
how they had spoken of it in whispers;
that once
having found no victim in the Hofgarten
he had

Kurten *raises his scissors.*

Wehner   he had cut
the head

The scissors come down. **Frau Kurten** *drops her head. Red light bathes the stage.*

from a sleeping swan
and drunk its gushing blood.

Lights fade.

XXXI: Epilogue

Wehner *comes forward.*

Wehner   In the years that followed Peter's execution
I
and a great many 'normal' men
were to do things we had never thought ourselves capable of.
I was lucky.
Before my hands got too bloody,
I fled from my homeland,
found a woman I love dearly
and had two beautiful children by her.
The law is no longer my concern.

Kurten *and* **Frau Kurten** *turn to face the audience.*

Wehner   I do not know if there is a God.
But if there is I know that
come the day of judgement
we will all go before him
saints and sinners alike
I can only hope that he will judge us
not as the monsters we have become

Frau Kurten, **Wehner** *and* **Kurten** *simultaneously:*

but as the children
we once were.

Lights fade on them, and for a moment, lights up on the swan. Lights fade.

End.

Penetrator

Penetrator was first performed at the Traverse Theatre, Edinburgh, on 12 August 1993. It transferred to the Finborough Theatre, London, later that year, and subsequently the Royal Court Theatre Upstairs, London, on 12 January 1994. The cast was as follows:

Tadge	James Cunningham
Max	Anthony Neilson
Alan	Alan Francis

Directed by Anthony Neilson
Designed by Michael T. Roberts

Characters

Tadge
Max
Alan

One

The sound of rain and the occasional passing car. A deep, ominous bass rumble.

A young man stands at the side of the road, thumb out. An army rucksack at his heel, like a patient dog. Rain stains his shoulders. His eyes are glazed. They widen as headlights bleach his features. He watches the car pass without stopping, his thumb dropping. The car disappears from sight. Slowly he faces the road again, raising his thumb once more. His actions are slow and dreamlike. Over this, a voice, deep and subhuman:

Voice-over 'Where are you going?' she asked. My luck was in. She may have been barely old enough to drive but she was pretty, and she had the dirtiest big tits I've ever seen on a girl. 'Same place as you' I said.

Another car approaches, the lights in his eyes, and passes as before.

I got into the car. My cock was like a truncheon in my jeans. I saw her looking at it, licking her sluttish red lips. 'But if I'm giving you a ride, you should do the same for me' she said, smiling.

Another car. It doesn't stop.

And then, to my amazement, she took of her T-shirt. Her nipples were like big stiff strawberries. 'You like them?' she asked, pulling on them hornily until she came. 'You dirty bitch' I said. 'You're really asking for it.'

Another car.

She hitched up her tiny skirt to reveal her gash, spreading the lips of her fuck-hole like some filthy tart, a flood of thick cunt juice cascading down her long legs. She sobbed with pleasure.

Another car approaches, the light on his face.

'Fuck me with your big tool' she moaned.

Unexpectedly the car stops. He watches it, his back to us.

I could see her tight pink arsehole now. 'Fuck my brains out' she gasped. 'Fuck me until I scream' she moaned.

And then the young man picks up his bag, and heads towards the car. He disappears into the night.

I want you to
I want you to shoot
I want you to shoot me

Darkness now. The bass rumble fades away.

Two

Lights up on the living-room of a rented flat. It is cheaply furnished, though someone with an eye for interior design has made the best of it. A coffee-table, however, overflows with junk. Posters of various icons on the wall. In this space, the credibly masculine fights with a softer influence. Damp on the walls near the roof, and the sound of distant traffic outside.

Max, *his back to us, is hunched on the floor. A pornographic magazine lies open before him.*

The pitch of the voice rises until it becomes recognisably human.

Voice-over   I want you to shoot me full of
your thick
of your thick salty cum
I want you to
shoot −

A tension goes out of him as he ejaculates. He assumes an almost foetal position, holding his sperm-covered palm away from himself. A long pause. He straightens, doing himself up and rolls into a sitting position, slumped against the settee. He stares at the semen in his hand, as if in a trance. The sound of traffic. A moment of peace.

Using some toilet roll, he wipes the semen from his hand, then discards the tissue. Pause. He sighs.

He gets up and walks to the window, looking out, perhaps singing to himself. He lights a fag, then returns to the settee. He sits down and resumes the game of Chinese patience he was playing, but he has no patience for it. He drinks some beer and unfolds a small packet of speed which he dabs from. His cigarette rolls off the ashtray and burns the table. He picks it up quickly but it's made a mark. He licks his finger and tries to rub the mark away but to no avail. He curses, then notices an odd taste in his mouth. He looks at the offending finger as the penny drops. The sound of his flatmate's key in the lock.

As if electrocuted he leaps up, grabbing the magazine. No time to hide it, so he stuffs it in his shirt and tries to look relaxed. **Alan** *enters, carrying a bin-liner full of laundry, and a small bag of shopping. They acknowledge each other with a nod.*

Max   Arsehole.

Alan   Fuckface. How's life?

Max   Shite. What's in the bag?

Alan   Take a wild guess.

Alan *has dumped the bag of washing and carries the small bag into the kitchen.* **Max** *stuffs the porn mag under the sofa cushion.*

Max   A four-pack of Rolos.

Alan (*off, as Brucie[1]*)   A four-pack of Rolos . . .

Max   Happy Shopper tea bags.

Alan (*off, as Brucie*)   Shopper tea bags, yes, *and* . . . ?

Max   A tin of Plumrose Bacon Grill.

Alan *reappears.*

Alan (*as Brucie*)   He's got the *lot*!

Max   Why don't you tell her?

Alan   I *do*.

Max   What does she say?

Alan   She says it never goes wrong.

Max   But you're a vegetarian.

Alan *starts to unload the washing, neatly folding each item and placing them in two piles.*

Alan   But you're not.

Max   There's still two tins left. You should never have said you liked it.

Alan   It *was* fifteen years ago.

Max   Mothers and Elephants never forget.

Alan   As soon as I get in, she's on at me to take my jacket off. You know me: I like to keep my jacket on, but no – (*Nagging voice.*) 'You won't feel the benefit when you go out again. You won't feel the benefit. You won't feel the benefit.' So I said to her in *that* case, surely when it's *summer*, I should put a jacket *on* when I get in, so that when I go *out* I can feel the benefit of taking it *off*. (*Pause.*) She couldn't answer *that*.

Max *nods, smiling at the familiarity of it.*

Max   As it was so shall it ever be.

Alan   Did you say *tea*?

Max (*smiles*)   Go *straight* to fuck. Do *not* pass go. Do *not* collect two hundred pounds.

Alan   Come on.

Max   I don't *want* any tea.

Alan   I didn't *want* to wash your shit-streaked pants.

Max   *You* didn't.

Alan   Come on.

Max   No.

Alan   That's three times in a row I've taken the washing . . .

Max   Did I *ask* you to?

Alan   . . . and you won't even make me a cup of *tea*!

Max That's because I'm an ungrateful *cunt*.

Alan *continues to unpack the clothes in silence. A long pause. Sighing demonstratively,* **Max** *gets up.*

Max (*angrily*) I'm *doing* it because if I *don't* you'll go in a fucking *huff* for the whole *night!*

He clumps into the kitchen.

I don't know why you can't just come out and *ask!*

Alan *smiles to himself.*

Max (*off*) There's no cups.

Alan Because they're all in *your* room.

Max (*off*) Are they fuck.

Pause. **Max** *crosses behind* **Alan**, *going to his room. Finding a pair of pants,* **Alan** *puts them on his head. Pause.* **Max** *crosses back to the kitchen behind* **Alan**, *carrying about six cups.*

Alan What about Baghdad²? Any more raids?

Max (*off*) Nah. Bunch of poofs.

Alan Where's the TV bit?

Max *doesn't answer. Pause.* **Alan** *stops what he's doing and wanders over to the settee. He looks around. He is about to lift the cushion under which the porno mag is hidden, when* **Max** *darts out of the kitchen behind him.*

Max I threw it out.

Alan *turns to look at him.*

Alan You threw it *out?*

Max (*nods*) Sorry. It was a mistake.

Alan A mistake?

Max (*nods*) I thought it was finished.

Pause. **Alan** *returns to the laundry.*

Alan You never throw anything out. There's three-month-old Chinese cartons in your room that you *still* haven't thrown out, and you throw out the *TV* bit . . .

Max *is back in the kitchen.*

Max (*off*)   There's fuck all on anyway.

Alan   Like what?

Max (*off*)   *Starsky and Hutch*[3] was on.

Alan (*sings theme tune, excitedly*)   Brilliant.

Max (*off*)   It was *shite.*

Alan   I used to *love Starsky and Hutch*!

Max (*off*)   So did *I.*

Alan   I had a friend and his whole room was *covered* in posters of Starsky and Hutch, and he had the little *car* and all the books and I was *jealous* of him. Totally *jealous.* I *refuse* to believe that *Starsky and Hutch* was shite.

Max (*off*)   *Rrrrüünnngg*!! This Is Your Wake-Up Call. It was *shite.* It was shite *then* and it's shite *now.* It was all shite. *The Persuaders, The Protectors, The Invaders, The Avengers, The* fucking *Waltons, Thunder-fucking-birds, The Man from Bollocks, The Hair-Bear Fucks, Mary Mungo and* fucking *Midge, all* of it − *shite.*

Alan (*pause*)   *Dr Who* was good. The Jon Pertwee ones.

Max   *Dr Who* was *shite,* for buck-toothed *fucks* in parkas.

Alan   *I* used to like it.

Max (*off*)   You *were* a buck-toothed fuck in a parka.

Alan   I thought *you* used to like it. (*Pause.*) You told me you *liked* it.

Max *emerges from the kitchen, carrying two cups of tea.*

Max   I *used* to like Creamola *Foam*[4], but when I walk into a *pub* I expect *beer.*

He sits down, placing the cups on the table. The tea bags are still in them.

If they'd just start bombing again we could have some *decent* telly.

Alan   You sick bastard.

Max   You'd prefer another (*Mock French.*) 'Alain Delon⁵' movie?

Alan   True enough.

He watches **Max** *squeeze the tea bags with his fingers.*

Ever heard of a teaspoon?

Max (*smiles*)   Don't be such a fucking *bumboy*. (*Pause.*) Besides, *this* way – not only do you get a nice strong *cuppa*, but it *also* cleans out all the . . . arsepickings that get trapped under your nails.

Alan *makes a face of disgust. Finished sorting the laundry, he indicates* **Max**'s *pile.*

Alan   One of your socks got shredded.

Max *nods.* **Alan** *sits down, reaching for his cup of tea.*

Alan   You *will* put that away?

Max *nods, starting to skin-up a joint. A long pause.*

Alan   Because you always say that and it just *sits* there . . .

Max   I *said* yes.

Alan (*pause*)   When?

Max (*sighs*)   In a *minute*.

A long pause.

Alan   Good night last night?

Max (*pause*)   Got stoned, got pissed, took some E, ate a kebab, puked *up* a kebab, I *presume* it was the same one (*Sighs.*), went to the Archers, got dragged along to Subsonic where I became as one with a faceless mass of space cadets dancing to a three-hour-long song which sounded like various international dialling tones and woke up at seven this morning in Mikey's toilet in a puddle of piss with speed cramps.

A pause. Simultaneously:

Alan/Max   It was a *great* night!!

They make much of this, laughing. A long pause.

Alan   Who was all there?

Max (*shakes head*)   The usual.
Mikey, obviously. Pete, the two Dougies, Malky. (*Pause.*) Drew, Pew, Barney McGrew, Cuthbert, Dibble . . .[6]

Alan   Grubb?

Max (*shakes head*)   No. Grubb was down the bandstand fucking Hambel up the shitter.

They smile.

Alan   What's Malky up to?

Max (*shakes head*)   What's anyone up to?

Alan *nods.* **Max** *sparks up the joint.*

Max   No, I tell a lie: you know Pete?

Alan (*in Pete's voice*)   *Pete!*

Max (*nods*)   Pete is selling his *jism* for fifty quid a shot.

A long pause.

Alan   It's amazing what tourists will buy.

Max (*nods, laughing*)   He tells them it's Robert Burns'.

They laugh.

No, seriously, fifty quid, the sperm bank. And what he *does* is: he sells some *here* and then gets the cheap bus over to Glasgow and sells some *there*. So that's a hundred undeclared quid a week for *two* hand-shandies.

A pause.

Alan   Makes you think.

Max (*nods. Pause*)   Enough to give *anyone* a pan-handle.

Alan (*in coarse voice*)   A knob like a wain's arm huddin a toffee apple.[7]

Max (*in same voice*)   A Jap's Eye like Moby Dick's blowhole!

Alan (*same*)   Boz like two plums stuck in a turkey's *throat*!

They have a good laugh. **Max** *passes* **Alan** *the joint. He draws on it, shuddering with the hit of it. A long pause.*

Game of cards?

Max (*pause*)   What?

Alan   Chinese patience?

Max   *Fuck* no. (*Pause.*) Scabby queen.

Alan   You thrash me at that. Something simple. Switch.

Max   Switch is for faggots.

Alan   Well, I'm a faggot then.

Max   I had my suspicions.

Alan   Do you want to play or not?

He nods, gathering up the cards and shuffling them flashily.

Max   If you lose the teddies fuck.

Alan (*smiles, shaking head*)   No they don't.

Max (*smiles, nodding*)   They do. They go at it like bunnies. Teddies, hung like donkeys, going at it like bunnies, doggy-style.

Alan   Fuck off.

Max *starts to deal.*

Note: The card game is now played out under the following dialogue. Such dialogue as comes up with regards to the game, can be interspersed with the following:

Alan   So did that girl go along then?

Max   Which?

Alan   Last night.

Max   Oh *fuck*.

Alan   She wasn't too impressed with *you* either.

Max   I'll live.

Alan   I didn't really hear it. What was she saying?

Max   Basically that because I use the word cunt, I'm a potential rapist.

Alan   She was offended.

Max   She didn't seem to mind using the word *dickhead*. (*Pause.*) She didn't seem to mind using the word *bastard*, and think about the meaning of *that*.

Alan   Yes but nobody uses that literally.

Max (*nods*)   The same with cunt. If I wanted to insult someone, why would I compare them to a vagina? It happens to be a part of the anatomy that I'm quite *fond* off, you know? (*Pause.*) No, it's bullshit. She was just another one of these fanny-bashers that Mikey collects so he can feel all right on.

Alan *furrows his brow at the 'fanny-basher' comment.*

Max   Don't *you* start. You *know* what I'm saying; I don't give a rat's arsehole what *anybody* does. But she's got fuck all to do with her time, so she's a professional *feminist*, just like Mel's a professional *poof*. I'm sick of these fuckers. What do they *want*? Because you can't *win* with these people. (*Pause.*) All men are bastards. Well I know plenty of men who were *nice* men, who were *good* men, until they got fucked over by *women*. *I* used to be a nice guy. Seriously. Where did it get me? *Nowhere*. (*Pause.*) Nowhere. (*Pause.*) I'll tell you something: Women will *always* get what they want. If they haven't *got* it yet, it's because not enough of them *want* it.

Alan (*pause*)   Or because not enough of them *know* they want it.

Max   Where did you read that? *Company*? In between 'How to banish cellulite' and 'The perfect blowjob'?

Alan   That's what I'm *saying*: that there are plenty of women who don't even ...

Max   Wait a minute. Wait a minute. How many women do you *know* exactly?

Alan   I know *plenty* of women.

Max   Plenty?

Alan (*nods*)   Plenty.

Max   Who?

Alan (*pause*)   You want me to *list* them?

Max   You know plenty of women as *friends*.

Alan (*pause*)   Not *just*.

Max   Because all this is *theory* ...

Alan   I'm not in a *relationship*, no, but I ...

Max   Come *on*. The last time *you* were out with a woman she was pushing you down the street in a fucking *pram*!

Alan   What are you trying to say?

Max   I'm not trying to say *anything*! You don't go in for that sort of thing ...

Alan   It's not that I don't go *in* for it ...

Max   But that's *fine*. I fucking *envy* you. All I'm saying is that a lot of stuff goes by the *wayside*.

Alan *says nothing. They go go on with the game in silence. Eventually:*

Max   You're in the fucking *huff*.

Alan   I'm not.

Max   You *are*, you humourless fucker.

Alan   I'm *not* in the huff.

They finish the game. **Alan** *is disinterested in its outcome. After a long pause,* **Max** *offers the small packet to* **Alan**:

Max   Spot of Billy?

Pause. **Alan** *shakes his head.*

Alan   I don't want to be up all night.

Max   Got to get up for work?

Alan *smiles sarcastically. A long pause. And then* **Max** *begins to sing.*

Max (*sings*)   On a mountain in Virginia,
There's a lonesome pine . . .

Smiling despite, himself, **Alan** *starts to join in. They have obviously done this before, because they have some nice harmonies worked out. Eventually, they are up and dancing around the room, adding whatever embellishments come naturally. They sing:*

Max/Alan (*sing*)   In the pale moonshine,
Our hearts entwine,
Where she carved her name
And I carved mine O June,
Like the mountains are blue,
Like the pine
I am lonesome for you

And perhaps **Max** *playfully clunks* **Alan** *over the head à la Laurel and Hardy.*

On
The
Blue Ridge Mountains of Virginia
On the trail of the lonesome Pine.

They finish with a flourish direct to the audience.

Lights fade.

Three

The same deep, ominous bass rumble as in Scene One.

Two neon signs light up. One says: 'GRILS GRILS GRILS'. The other: 'VILE BED SHOW'.

They flash on and off. The young traveller stands beneath them, bag in hand. He stares up, his back to the audience. Over this, as before:

Voice-over *Oooh.* Oooh *yeah.* That's how you like it. You like it that way, don't you? You like that cock up your ass, don't you? Up that tight little *ass.*

The frame of a window lights up. This is what the young man is staring up at. The silhouette of a figure stands at the window, looking out.

Tighten that ass you little *bitch.* You little rent-boy bitch. You like to take it all, don't you? All that prick. You like that prick, don't you? You *love* that prick.

The young man's knuckles whiten as he squeezes the straps of his bag.

We're going to fill every hole you've *got.* Oooh *yeah.* We're going to fill you up.

The light fades on the young man, leaving only the window.

We're going to shoot you
Shoot you full
Shoot you.

Four

Lights fade up on the living-room. **Alan** *stands at the window, looking out (immediately recognisable as the silhouette).*

Lights fade down on the window.

Max *is nowhere to be seen, but on the back of the settee, two ragged soft toys are simulating copulation. The voice-over fades out to be replaced by* **Max***'s voice, from behind the settee.*

Max Shoot you full you puppet *fuck.* Oooh. Oooh yeah.

Yeah. Tighten that puppet butt. That soft-toy *butt.*

Alan *looks at them, his brow furrowed but smiling nonetheless.*

Alan   But I *won.* I don't see how the teddies fuck when I *won.*

Max *pops his head over the back of the couch.*

Max   This is getting me *hot.* These are a couple of *hot* teddies you've got here. I don't know how you ever got any sleep.

Alan   I think the teddies have had enough now.

Max   Do you think so?

Alan (*in Brucie voice*)   I *think* they've *had enough!*

Max   Because I was getting so horny there I felt like joining in.

Smiling evilly, he makes threats to unzip his flies and sodomise one of the teddies. After a good-natured tussle, **Alan** *manages to wrest the teddies from* **Max**'s *grasp.*

You're too sentimental. The teddies like to fuck.

Alan   They *don't.*

Max   What do you think they *do* on their picnics? After the food's gone and they're tanked up on Bucky? They're beasts of the wild.

Alan   They're *not* beasts of the wild. They're part of the family.

Max   Families are *built* on fucking. Fucking and secrets. (*Pause.*) When I became a man, I put away childish things.

Alan   You didn't put *anything* away. You *gave* that giraffe thing to Laura and she set *fire* to it.

Pause. **Max** *goes back to the settee, sits down, drinks some more beer and starts to roll another joint.* **Alan** *sits the teddies down, somewhere safe. He sits down too.*

Alan   I'm sorry.

Max (*nods*) It's all right.

Alan It just slipped out.
Pause.

(*As Roger Moore.*) It just slipped out, Moneypenny.

Max (*also as Moore*) Do you want a photie?

Alan (*Moore*) Are you looking at my bird? (*Pause.*) Square goes.

They laugh. Pause. A long pause.

Max She's a slut, you know that?

Pause. **Alan** *doesn't reply.*

It's hard for me to admit that, but she is. I'm not condoning the word 'slut' but it exists, and she fits the bill.

A long pause. **Max** *looks at* **Alan**.

Isn't she?

Alan I can't really comment. I don't know the full story.

Max You know enough.

Alan (*pause*) You haven't exactly been faithful to *her*, though, have you?

Max No. I *admit* that. I've made some mistakes in the past. It doesn't excuse *her* though, does it?

Pause. **Alan** *says nothing.*

She was crazy about me when I wasn't crazy about her and then when I *do* decide to *plunge* in, she goes cold. After all the *grief* she gave me, she throws me aside, she tells me 'We don't have any *fun*, it's all so *heavy*.' (*Pause.*) Women, you see, I'll tell you something: They use men – we use *them* too but in a different way – *They* use men to *learn*. I know how that sounds but they *do*. To *learn*. And when they've learnt as much as they can from you, they move on to the *next* sorry idiot. (*Pause.*) Besides, it's not as bad for a woman as it is for a man.

Pause. **Alan** *looks at him.*

Infidelity.

Alan (*pause*)   How do you figure that?

Max   It just *isn't*. In terms of society.

He lights the joint.

She knew *nothing* about sex when I met her. *Nothing*. She was Mary-fucking-Poppins when I met her and Mary-fucking-Millington when she *left* me.

Alan (*pause*)   Who?

Max   Mary Millington. She was a porno star in the 70s.

Alan (*nods*)   I wouldn't know.

Max   No. I don't really, either. (*Pause.*) But I know men. I know what's in their minds. (*Pause.*) And the pictures I get . . .

He shudders.

I don't want to talk about it. She's nothing to do with me. (*Pause.*) She's in the past.

He takes another swig of beer. A long pause. And then the door bell rings. They look at each other, horrified.

Alan   Who's that?

Max   *I* don't know, do I? I haven't got X-ray fucking eyes!

Alan   Are you expecting anybody?

Max *shakes his head.*

Max   Answer it, then.

Alan   *You* answer it.

Max (*pause*)   What if it's Laura?

They stare at each other. Pause.

You answer it.

Alan I *always* have to answer it!

It rings again.

Max Go on. I'll be your best pal.

He gets up, sighing.

Alan Hide that joint.

Max *conceals it with his hand.* **Alan** *stops halfway.*

Alan What if it *is* Laura? Are you in?

Max (*shakes head*) *No*!

Alan *turns to the door.*

Max *Yes*!

Alan *turns back to him again, looking exasperated.*

Max (*pause*) No. I'm not in. No.

Sighing, he goes to the door. **Max** *sits forward, listening intently. The door opens. Muffled voices in the hall. And then* **Alan** *re-enters, his eyes flaring at* **Max** *and rolling heavenwards. Behind him follows the young man.* **Max** *stands, surprised.*

Max Tadge!

Tadge *nods, taking in the room.* **Alan** *sits down.*

Max What the fuck are *you* doing here?

Max *is smiling now. He extends his hand.* **Tadge** *shakes it.*

Tadge All right man.

Max (*shakes head*) You squaddie bastard. Are you on leave?

Tadge *says nothing, looking round.* **Max** *sees blood on* **Tadge**'s *jacket.*

Max What the fuck's this? Are you all right?

Tadge *looks at the blood on his jacket. A long pause.*

Tadge It's all right man. It's not mine.

Max's *enthusiasm has waned slightly. Pause.*

Max   Sit down then. Take the weight off your cock.

Tadge (*pause*)   Off ma what?

Max (*pause*)   Just sit the fuck down. (*Smiles.*) You want some tea?

Tadge *nods, sitting down beside* **Alan** *on the settee. He looks at* **Alan**. **Alan** *gets up.*

Alan   I'll make some.

He picks up the cups from the table and goes into the kitchen. **Max** *sits down, passing* **Tadge** *the joint. He looks at it for a moment before accepting it. Pause.*

Max   It's good to see you. It's been a long time.

Tadge *stares in the direction that* **Alan** *went.*

Tadge   He looks different.

Max (*pause*)   Alan?

Tadge *nods.*

Tadge   He's lost weight.

Max (*pause. Nods*)   I can't tell.

A long pause.

So – how's the army life? See the world, meet new people, blow their brains out and all that?

Tadge *stares blankly ahead for a while, and then it is as if he rejoins reality.*

Tadge   I've been discharged.

Max (*pause*)   Discharged? (*Pause.*) What for?

Tadge (*pause*)   They're going to pay me eighty thousand pounds.

He looks at **Max** *as if he can hardly believe it himself.*

Max (*pause*)   Eighty *thousand*?

Pause. **Tadge** *nods. He looks in* **Alan***'s direction again.*

Tadge   His hair's shorter too.

Pause. **Max** *looks in that direction too.*

Max (*nods*)   Probably. (*Pause.*) But tell me about this eighty fucking *grand*! Are we in the money or what? You still *owe* me five grand.

Tadge *looks at him.*

Max   You bet me five grand that Ally's Tartan Army would win the World Cup, remember? A bet's a bet.

Alan *comes in.* **Tadge** *looks at him.*

Tadge   Alan?

Alan *nods an acknowledgement.*

Tadge   Have you had your hair cut?

Pause. **Alan** *looks puzzled.*

Alan   Not recently.

A long pause.

Max   But maybe since you last saw Tadge.

Alan (*pause. Nods*)   Probably.

Tadge   It suits you.

Pause. **Alan** *nods.*

Alan   D'you take sugar?

Pause. **Tadge** *looks at* **Max**.

Max   You *used* to take about four.

Pause. **Tadge** *looks back at* **Alan**.

Tadge   Four.

Pause. **Alan** *nods and goes back into the kitchen.* **Tadge** *is lost in space again.*

Max   Fill me *in*, then. What's going on? (*Pause.*) Do your folks know you're back?

Tadge (*pause*)   Have you seen my dad?

Max   Ronnie? (*Pause. Shakes his head.*) Not for years.

A long pause.

Tadge   He's not my dad.

Max *stares at him. Pause.*

Max   Ronnie's not your dad? (*Pause.*) How do you know?

Tadge *stares at him.*

Max   Did your mum tell you this?

Tadge (*pause*)   It was in my file. I saw it written in my file. They know everything about everybody. It was in my file.

Pause. **Alan** *comes in with the tea.* **Tadge** *watches him.* **Alan** *gives each of them a cup. There's no place to sit but beside* **Tadge**. **Tadge** *stares at him.* **Alan** *shifts uncomfortably.* **Max** *is at a loss.*

Max (*pause*)   But you *look* like Ronnie. Everyone's always said. (*Pause.*) Have you asked your mum about it? (*Pause.*) She *is* your mother though?

Pause. **Tadge** *says nothing.* **Max** *looks at* **Alan**.

Tadge found out that his dad isn't really his dad.

Alan   Isn't really his dad? (*Pause. Nods.*)

Tadge *gets up. They look up at him.*

Tadge   Toilet.

Alan (*indicating*)   First on the left.

Tadge *hovers there, not moving.*

Tadge (*to* **Alan**)   Can you show me?

Pause. **Alan** *looks at him, not knowing what to say.*

Max   First on the left, Tadge. You can't miss it. If your piss sounds dull, you're in a bedroom.

Pause. **Tadge** *exits.* **Max** *looks at* **Alan**.

Did you ever meet Ronnie?

Alan *shakes his head.*

Max   Tadge is the spitting image of him.

He looks in the direction of the toilet.

He's acting really strange.

Alan (*whispers loudly*)   What do you expect? He's a fucking *squaddie*!

Max   He's Tadge before that.

Alan   That's where you're *wrong*. You didn't see him the *last* time he was through! He's been totally *brainwashed*! He's been out there learning to *kill* people!

Max *makes a scoffing sound.* **Alan** *shakes his head.*

Alan   I've no time for him. I'm sorry. He's turned into a *fascist*!

Max   *Bollocks*!

Alan   Well, he hasn't been learning how to love God and furry animals, has he? (*Shakes head.*) He's been learning how to hate niggers and queers and Irish people and Arabs! He's been learning how to *bayonet* people for Christ's sake!!

Max (*sings naively*)   War is *stoo*-pid and *pee*-puhl are *stoo*pid[8] . . .

Alan (*indicates jacket*)   What about all that then? 'It's not mine'??! (*He covers his eyes. Calmly.*) As far as *I'm* concerned, when you *join* the *Army* you *forfeit* your *right* to be treated as a human being!

Max   Well, *that's* fucking tolerant of you!

Alan   *Tolerant*?!

Max   Look. Look. I *know*, and it was a fucking in*sane* thing to do I *agree* – but there were many reasons why he joined up and he's been dis*charged* now and he's obviously a bit fucked-up about this *news*. He's our *friend*.

Alan   Speak for yourself.

Max   What?

Alan   I've only known him a few years.

Max   You've only known *me* a few years.

Alan   But I hardly know him at all. You've got a history with him. I don't.

Max (*pause*)   I can't believe you're saying that.

Alan *says nothing. Pause. The toilet door opens and* **Tadge** *comes back in and sits down. Pause.*

Max   So did this file say who your real father *is*?

Tadge *has buried his face in his hands. Pause.*

Tadge   Can I stay the night?

Alan *glares at* **Max**, *'no'.*

Max   Uh . . . (*Pause.*) Yeah. Of course, man.

He glares back at **Alan**.

Of course you can.

Alan *shifts loudly.* **Tadge** *raises his head.*

Tadge   There was a guy in my thingmy, guess what he did?

He looks at them both. They can't guess.

Dying on a fuck, guess what he did, he chored some liver from the kitchens, raw liver and he fucked it into his thermos and shagged that and he was in the bunk by me and every night he was like that with his flask and he didn't change the liver for *three months*, man, and it gave him some fucking, like, *disease* that made his cock drip *pus* and that and when the CO found out they gave him a fucking *beauty* of a beasting.

Tadge *stares at them, smiling, looking quite mad. A long pause.*

Alan   A beasting?

Tadge *is staring at him. Pause.*

Tadge   What was that?

He stares intently at him. **Alan** *shifts again. He shakes his head.*
Tadge *just continues to stare at him, as if trying to puzzle
something out. A long pause.*

Alan   What?

Pause.

Max   So tell us more about all this . . .

Tadge (*to* **Alan**)   Do you smell something?

Alan (*pause*)   Eh?

Tadge   You're looking at me like you do.

Max   Look . . .

Tadge   Have you got a problem?

Alan (*pause*)   Not with you, Tadge.

Tadge   Who with then?

Alan (*a long pause*)   The army.

Max   For fuck's *sake*!

Alan (*to* **Max**)   Well it's *true*.

Tadge   Would you like it if Saddam Hussein was running
the country?

Alan   Of *course* not . . .

Tadge (*shakes head*)   We know everything about him.
We've got stuff you wouldn't believe. We could kill him
any time we like without going anywhere near him.

Pause.

Max   So why don't we?

Tadge   Top secret.

Max   You can't tell us?

Tadge (*pause*)   I don't know. (*Pause. He stares at* **Max**.) They're going to give me twenty thousand pounds.

Max (*pause*)   I thought it was eighty?

Tadge *stares at him, uncomprehending.*

Max   Are you feeling all right?

A long pause.

Tadge   I'm in trouble, man. They've been following me.

Max (*pause*)   Who has?

Tadge (*pause*)   The Penetrators.

A long pause. **Max** *looks at* **Alan**, *who shrugs, intrigued.*

Max   The Penetrators?

Pause. **Tadge** *nods. Muffled sounds from next door's telly.*

Tadge   It goes right to the top. I found them out. They wanted me to join but I wouldn't and now they want me dead.

Alan   *Dead*?

Tadge (*nods. Pause*)   They'll find me and they'll kill me so I can never tell. And then they'll destroy all my files like I was never here. They can do that. That's how powerful they are. They can make it so you were never here.

Alan   But *we* know, Tadge.

Tadge (*pause*)   Maybe they'll kill you too.

Pause. **Alan** *looks at* **Max**.

Alan   Did he say what I *think* he said?

Max *nods.*

Max   What the fuck do they *do*, these . . . terminators or whatever?

Tadge   Penetrators.

Max   Penetrators.

Tadge   They penetrate.

Alan   Ask a silly question.

Max   What they're an . . . undercover unit or . . . ?

Tadge *shakes his head.*

Tadge   They stick things up you. (*Pause.*) Up your arse.

Max   Up your *arse*?

Tadge   They stick things up you. All sorts of things. I found out about them and they kept me in this . . . black room, it was a . . . just a black room. They drugged me. I never saw their faces. They'd bring me round every now and then so they could do more things to me. It must have been weeks. I don't know how long. Maybe months.

A long pause.

Alan   It doesn't surprise me.

Max   It *doesn't*?

Alan (*shakes head*)   I've heard stories like that before. We don't know half of what goes on in these places. It's what I was saying.

Max   But you escaped . . . ?

Tadge   I only pretended to take my pills. I waited for them in the black room. Three of them came this time. They had a wooden pole. They were going to stick it up me.

He stands, trying to remember. He begins to half-act the events as if they are not clear in his mind and he seeks to clarify them.

They told me to . . . bend over . . . ?

Which he does.

So I bent over but then I . . .

*He looks around, then at **Alan**.*

Alan, you be the guy.

*Pause. **Alan** looks at him.*

Alan   I'm having a cup of tea . . .

Tadge *gently pulls him up.*

Tadge   I won't hurt you.

Alan *looks at* **Max** *who reassures him. Reluctantly, he allows*
Tadge *to manipulate him.* **Tadge** *bends over, positioning* **Alan**
behind him.

Tadge   So I'm bent over. Alan, pretend you've got a
pole.

Max   That won't be easy.

Alan *smiles sarcastically.*

Alan   What do you mean?

Tadge   Pretend you've got a pole and you're going to
stick it up me.

Feeling foolish, **Alan** *does so. Slowly,* **Tadge** *goes through the
motions.*

I swung round . . .

Alan (*as Brucie*)   Swung round, right . . .

Tadge   I grabbed the pole . . .

Alan (*as Brucie*)   The *pole*, right . . .

Tadge   And I –

He mimes snapping the pole over his leg. A sharp movement.

snapped it in half . . .

Alan (*as Brucie*)   In *half*, love, for God's sake . . .

Max *is laughing at this.*

Tadge   And then I –

*Quickly he spins round, jabbing at **Alan**'s eye.*

In his eye –

Alan *flinches.*

Tadge   And –

*Another quick movement and he grabs **Alan** by the hair. **Alan** yelps and **Max** stops laughing.*

Got the other one and –

*He jerks **Alan**'s head back. He croaks. **Tadge** mimes striking his throat with the pole three times. Each blow comes dangerously close.*

like this and there was a sound and –

*He forces **Alan** to his knees. This all happens in seconds.*

the third one on the floor and –

*He twists **Alan**'s hair until he rolls onto his back.*

WHACK!

Max *jumps at the shout.* **Tadge** *mimes hitting **Alan** in the balls with the pole.* **Alan** *reacts instinctively to each.*

Tadge   WHACK! on the balls
WHACK! calling him a fucking poof
WHACK!
WHACK!
WHACK! and there was blood on him
WHACK! WHACK! WHACK! WHACK!
WHACK!

*And then he stops, breathless, standing over **Alan** who looks up at him fearfully. For a long time he stares down at him.*

He stopped moving. Stopped breathing. (*Pause.*) I got out, over the fence. I got to the road. I came here.

Pause. **Tadge** *returns to his seat.* **Max** *is speechless.* **Alan** *picks* *himself up. Pause.*

Alan   I'm going to make some more tea.

Pause. **Max** *nods.* **Alan** *goes to the kitchen with the cups.* **Max** *and* **Tadge** *sit in silence.* **Tadge** *looks at him.*

Tadge   Did you know?

Max   About your dad? (*Pause.*) No. I still can't believe it.

Pause.

Tadge   So you didn't ... (*Long pause.*) ... come and visit me, did you?

Max (*pause*)   Visit you?

Tadge (*nods. Pause*)   In the barracks. You and my dad.

Pause. Troubled, **Max** *shakes his head.* **Tadge** *looks frightened. He looks in* **Alan***'s direction.*

Tadge   Does he have a girlfriend?

Pause. **Max** *shakes his head.*

Why not?

Pause. He looks at **Max***, who shrugs.*

I saw Malky the other day.

Max (*pause*)   Did you?.

Tadge (*pause*)   He had a knife. He said I owed him money. He said he was going to stab me up the arse.

He looks at **Max***. A long pause.* **Max** *picks up the pack of cards.*

Max   Tadge.

Pause. **Tadge** *looks at him.* **Max** *proceeds to show him a card trick.*

Note: This should be a trick of illusion.

When it is done **Tadge** *stares at the cards for a time. He looks at* **Max***, an awful horror in his eyes. Pause.*

Tadge It's not real, is it?

Pause. **Alan** *comes in with the tea, distributes it as before.* **Tadge** *watches him.*

Tadge Have you lost weight?

Alan *looks at him, not knowing what to say.*

Tadge (*pause*) Suits you. (*Pause.*) I shagged two girls at once.

He looks at them both for encouragement. They look depressed.

I did. In West Germany on the base. Two of them, about thirteen years old each.

Pause. **Max** *nods.*

But I can have anything I want see. On account of my dad.

Alan I thought you didn't know who he was.

Tadge *nods.*

Max Who?

Tadge (*pause*) Norman Schwarzkopf[9].

A long pause. **Alan** *smiles.*

Alan Stormin' Norman?

Tadge *nods. They can't help smiling.* **Tadge** *smiles too, almost delighted.*

Tadge Seriously. I found it all out. My mum was over in America before she had me. That's when it happened. That's why they were filming me. To blackmail him.

As he gets more energetic their smiles fade.

That's why they're giving me half a million pounds.

He looks at them. Silence. **Tadge***'s smile fades too. He gets up.*

Tadge Can I go and lie down for a while?

Pause. **Max** *nods.*

Max   My room's through there.

Tadge *looks in the indicated direction. Then he looks at* **Alan**.

Tadge   Which one's yours?

Alan (*pause*)   Second on the left.

Tadge *exits. They wait until he has got down the hall, then they both exhale heavily. They talk in loud whispers.*

Alan   *He* is *off* his *nut*!

Max *gestures for him to be quieter.*

Alan   *He* is a *psychopath*! And *we* have him *staying* in our *house*! And *we* are never going to get *rid* of him!

Max   What the fuck am I supposed to do?! Throw him out?! He'll end up *killing* himself!

Alan   So we keep him here and he kills *us*?!

Max   Don't talk *shite*!

Alan   How do you know *what* he'll do?!

Max   Because I *know* him!

Alan   No! *Him* you do *not* know! *He* is a . . .

Tadge *comes back in. They stop talking immediately. He stares at them for a moment then bends down to pick up his bag. He turns and leaves. Again they wait for him to get to the room.*

Alan   We should call a *doctor* that's what we should do!

He taps at his temple.

A *doctor*!

Max   Shut up a minute, will you?

Alan   His father at least.

Max *shakes his head.*

Alan   Why *not*?!

Max   We can't.

Alan You don't have the number?

Max (*shakes head*) It's not that. We just can't call him. He's not one of those people you *call*, all right?

Alan What do you mean he's not one of . . .

Max (*shakes head*) It's *not* an option.

Alan *sits down. Pause.*

Max *Something* must have happened to him. (*Pause.*) Maybe he *did* find out he was adopted. Maybe that's true.

Alan And it just freaked him out?

Max (*nods*) Or maybe there's some truth in this Penetrator thing.

Alan (*nods*) An initiation thing.

Max Or an actual rape. It's bound to happen.

Alan (*nods*) Maybe it wasn't even rape. Maybe he consented.

Max (*pause*) Consented? I can't see it myself. (*Pause.*) But it might have been something less *serious* than rape . . .

Alan (*nods*) In the showers, an incident, that he's blown up in his mind.

Pause. They smile.

There's a joke in there somewhere.

Max That's why he's called Tadge. Did you know that?

Alan (*smiling, shaking head*) No . . .?

Max (*nods, smiling*) He was the hard-nut of primary five. So because he was the hard-nut of primary five, he was picked on by all the hard-nuts of primary seven.

Alan What about the hard-nuts of primary six?

Max No, he could take them.

Alan *nods.*

Max   So we were all in the showers after swimming and these primary seven boys came in looking for him.

Alan   Didn't they get soaked?

Max   (*shakes head*)   They were next in the pool so they had their . . .

He indicates swimwear. **Alan** *nods.*

Anyway they were all dancing round him like twats, gobbing and slapping him with towels, snapping the elastic on his trunks, all that stuff. There were too many of them to do anything. Anyway – just one of those things, hot water, blood pumping – he got a . . .

Indicates erection. **Alan** *winces.*

Alan   A woody?

Max   (*smiles, nodding*)   A *plank.*

Pause. **Alan** *shakes his head.*

Alan   A stonker in the showers. (*Laughs.*) Nothing worse.

Max   (*nods. Pause*)   So when they saw *this* . . . A fucking *gift.* Pissing themselves, pointing, chanting, and there he was in the corner. But it wouldn't go down. It just stayed there.

Alan *shakes his head. Pause.*

Max   So people started calling him Tadger, behind his back at first, because he tried to beat up anyone who did, but sheer weight of numbers won out, and it just stuck through secondary until nobody remembered how it had ever started.

Alan   Apart from you.

Max   Apart from me. (*Pause.*) But it worked out OK because by fourth year all the girls thought he was called Tadge because he had such a *big* one.

Pause.

Alan   Best days of your life.

Max Fuck that. (*Pause.*) First time I ever met him, I was
five years old, I had a toy rifle. He asked me for a shot
but I said no, and he punched me in the fucking *gob*.
(*Smiles.*) Naturally we became great friends, and many
Chinese burns and deadlegs have passed under the bridge
since then.

Alan (*pause*) Why'd you put up with that?

Max (*pause. Shrugs*) I didn't know I was putting up with
anything.

Alan (*nods*) We used to have this thing called plugging . . .

Max *Plugging?*

Alan (*nods*) There was a whole process to it. Someone
would be accused of a heinous crime – like being *fat* or
getting a good exam mark. You'd then be appointed a
defence. Prosecution would make its case, like they'd pull
up your shirt and say 'Look at him, he's a fat bastard' and
then your defence would answer the charges. The problem
was that your defence lawyer was as eager to see you
plugged as everyone else. I don't remember a single verdict
of not guilty.

Pause.

So you'd then be taken behind the big drums with all the
scrap food in them, and summarily plugged, which basically
involved someone getting a firm grip on your meat and
two veg and . . . *twisting* them round as far as they'd go.

*It's **Max**'s turn to wince.*

Fucking sore actually.

A long pause.

Max Maybe we should call the army?

Alan No *way*! They'd tell us nothing and we'd have
Military Police at the door in *seconds*, and *they* are *total*
bastards. (*Pause.*) And what if he's telling the *truth*? Imagine
if something that bizarre happened – nobody'd believe you.

They'd think what we think – that you were mad. Maybe they *would* kill us all.

Max *shakes his head.*

Alan   We don't know *half* of what goes on.

Max (*shakes head*)   No. He's fucked. (*Pause.*) I know he is.

A long pause. They start to smile.

Alan   Stormin' Norman.

Max   No *wonder* they stuck things up his arse.

Alan (*Southern drawl*)   I'm lookin' fur ma boy.

Max   I've got this picture of his mother fucking Stormin' Norman . . .

Alan (*Southern*)   OK ma'am, how about we look at some scuds and then I'll show you that Patriot Missile I was telling you about. We might even have time for a quick pincer movement . . .

They laugh.

Lights fade on them.

Five

Darkness.
Deep ominous bass.
The sound of laughter through walls.
A multitude of voices whispering frantically, passing secrets, telling lies.
Somewhere in the dark, **Tadge** *listens, his eyes wide.*
Eventually, the sounds fade away and the lights fade back up to:

Six

Alan *and* **Max** *as before, but in the aftermath of laughter. Pause.*

Max   We shouldn't laugh. It's not funny.

Alan   No. I *know* it isn't. There's a deranged *soldier* in my bed!

Max   Your lucky day.

Alan (*pause*)   Why do you say things like that?

Max   Like what?

Alan   Like that.

Max   Like fucking *what*?

Alan   You're always saying things like that.

Max   It was a joke.

Alan   You make an awful lot of them.

Max   Does it worry you?

Alan   It obviously worries *you*.

Max   Doesn't worry me at *all*.

Alan   Yes it does.

Max   *What?*

Alan   What?

Max   What should I worry about?

Alan   Nothing.

Max   Nothing then. (*Pause.*) Skin up.

Pause. **Alan** *grudgingly starts to assemble a joint.* **Max** *wanders over to the tape deck, sifts through the tapes.*

Alan   Putting a tape on?

Max (*nods. Pause*)   Why?

Alan   I was enjoying the silence. (*Pause.*) We don't want to wake him up.

Max *is looking at a tape.*

Max   What's on this?

He hold sit up for **Alan** *to see.* **Alan** *shakes his head.*

Alan   Must be one of yours.

Max *looks at it again and puts the tape in. A moment's silence before the song starts. They wait expectantly. It begins.*

Note: Any song can play here, possibly even changing from night to night. The only proviso is that it should have some nostalgic quality, a well-known song that we have forgotten we knew and one that would have been familiar to **Max** *and* **Alan**'s *generation. It should also, for apparent reasons, be in some way danceable.*

After a few bars, **Max** *and* **Alan** *recognise the song.* **Alan** *stops what he is doing and they dance around the room to it or mime to it or whatever, as silly as you like. This goes on for some two-thirds of the song and then, unseen by* **Alan** *at least,* **Tadge** *enters, carrying his bag. He watches* **Alan**. *When* **Alan** *sees him there, he becomes self-conscious and gradually the dance fades.* **Max** *turns off the tape. Pause.* **Alan** *returns to his seat.*

Max (*to* **Tadge**)   How are you feeling?

Pause. **Tadge** *looks at him and nods.*

Did you get some sleep?

Pause. **Tadge** *doesn't answer. He crosses to the settee and sits beside* **Alan**, *holding his bag on his knee and staring ahead.*

Max (*pause*)   More tea?

Tadge *looks at him.*

Alan   *No.*

Alan *glares at him.*

Max   Tadge?

Alan (*if looks could kill . . .*)   No thanks. (*Pause.*) I might make some *later.*

Alan *looks at him. He twigs. Pause.* **Max** *sits down. A long pause. Almost robotically,* **Tadge** *turns his head to look at* **Alan**. **Alan** *feels his gaze but concentrates on the joint he is rolling. A long pause* [10].

Max   What about *Jurassic Park* then. Heard it was a lot of *shite*.

Pause. **Alan** *clears his throat nervously. Silence.*

Max   Imagine if you had a fetish for shagging dinosaurs.

A long pause.

You'd be pretty *fucked*, wouldn't you? (*Pause.*) Personally, my fetish is that I can only achieve erection with women that look like Tiger from *The Double Deckers*. Remember her?

Tadge   Alan?

Alan *looks at him.*

Tadge   I couldn't sleep in there.

Alan (*pause*)   You couldn't sleep.

Tadge   I could hear things.

Alan (*pause*)   You could *hear* things?

Max   What kind of things?

Pause. **Tadge**'s *eyes glaze over. Pause. He looks at* **Max**.

Tadge   I feel a bit . . . funny.

Max (*pause*)   What *kind* of funny?

Long pause. **Tadge** *looks at* **Alan**.

Tadge   *Have* you got a girlfriend?

Alan *doesn't answer.* **Tadge** *looks at* **Max**.

Tadge   *Has* he?

Max   *I* don't fucking know.

Tadge *looks at* **Alan**.

Tadge   You *have*. That lassie, Laura.

Pause.

Max   No, that was me.

Tadge *looks at him, puzzled.* **Max** *nods.* **Tadge** *looks at* **Alan**.

Tadge (*pause*)   So you *haven't*?

Alan (*pause*)   Why do you want to know?

Max   He fucking *hasn't*, right?

Alan *looks at him.*

Max   What's the big fucking deal?

Tadge *looks at* **Max**.

Tadge   Why hasn't he?

Max (*pause*)   How the fuck should *I* know?

A long pause. **Tadge** *is blank, and then his brow furrows.*

Tadge   They kept me in . . . a black room. They hid me away. I never saw . . . their faces. (*Pause.*) They wore . . . gloves . . . ? (*Pause.*) They can make you disappear. Like a black hole. A black hole where a person was.

He looks at **Max**.

You don't believe me.

Max (*pause*)   I don't know what to believe, Tadge.

Tadge   Don't *call* me that! I don't want to be *called* that any more!

Max (*pause*)   That's fine by me.

Tadge   It's not my *name*!

Max (*nods*)   I know. (*Pause.*) I won't call you it again. I'll call you Ronnie.

Tadge   *That's* not my name either!

Max (*pause*)   Not Ronnie *Junior*!?

Tadge   *No*! That's *not* my *name*!

Max   Keep you're fucking *pants* on! What *is* your name?

Tadge (*pause*)   I don't know, *do* I? I don't *have* a name!

A long pause.

Alan Schwarzkopf, I suppose.

Tadge *stares at him.* **Alan** *shifts uncomfortably. He looks at* **Max**.

Alan If Stormin' Norman's his dad, his name must be Schwarzkopf, mustn't it?

Tadge (*pause*) Were *you* in the black room?

Alan (*pause*) Was *I*?

Tadge *nods. Pause.*

Alan No. Not me.

Tadge *You* believe me though, eh?

Alan (*pause*) I believe that *something* happened to you in there. I don't know *what*.

Tadge (*pause*) One of them, he put his arm up my arse, right up to *here*.

He indicates his elbow. Looks at **Max**.

Max That's impossible.

Tadge (*shakes head*) They made me sniff those poppers. It makes your arsehole loose.

Max (*pause*) It'd have to be pretty-fucking-*loose*. (*Pause.*) I don't know: I had a nurse trying to stick a thermometer up my arse once. (*Tightens his mouth.*) No Fucking Way. Felt like she was trying to get an *oar* up my Gary. (*Pause.*) And there was a younger nurse there too, and she kept glancing at my fucking dick. Really embarrassing. I wasn't exactly at my most . . . *manly* shall we say.

Alan (*nods, smiling*) Last cockle in the jar?

Max (*nods*) Like the tie-off on a *balloon*. (*Smiles.*) Fuck.

Tadge *is staring at him, wide-eyed. Pause.*

Tadge Remember when we found that scuddy in the Dell?

Pause. **Max** *nods, smiling.*

Tadge (*pause*)   It was soaking wet, eh?

Max *nods. Pause.*

Tadge   We took it to your house. Dried it out by the fire.

Max *nods. Pause.*

Tadge   And there was an old wifey in it that looked like Mrs Taylor, eh?

Max (*pause*)   Who was Mrs Taylor?

Tadge (*pause*)   She gave me those special lessons.

Max (*nods*)   Reading.

Tadge *nods. Pause.*

Tadge   And we both had a wank, eh?

A pregnant pause. **Alan** *looks embarrassed.* **Max** *clears his throat.* **Tadge** *looks at* **Alan**.

He'd never had a wank before. I showed him what to do.

Grinning innocently, he looks back at **Max**.

You almost shit yourself when you saw your spunk, eh?

Max   Aw, do we *have* to, man? It *was* a long time ago.

A long pause.

Tadge   It was a good laugh, though, eh?

Max (*pause*)   It was a long time ago.

Pause. **Tadge** *looks at* **Alan**.

Tadge   Do *you* think I'm thick?

Alan (*pause*)   Sick or thick?

Tadge   *Thick. Thick. You* must be the thick one!

Alan   I *don't* think you're thick.

A long pause.

Tadge   I'm not so thick I don't know a Penetrator when I see one.

Alan   What?

Pause. **Tadge** *stares at him, then looks away. Pause.* **Alan** *looks at* **Max**.

Alan   He's freaking me out a bit, Max. (*Pause.*) I'm a bit stoned and he's freaking me out.

Max *makes a gesture 'calm down'.*

Tadge   I can prove it to you.

He looks at them. Pause.

I took something off one of them.

Max (*pause*)   What?

Tadge *delves into the bag on his lap and almost immediately produces a big, ugly hunting knife: a knife to end all knives.* **Max** *and* **Alan** *are visibly taken aback.*

Alan   *Fuck*!

Max   Fuck's *sake*!!

Tadge *holds it proudly, looking at it.*

Tadge   I took it off one of them. He was going to stab me up the arse with it.

Alan (*shakes head*)   No way. No way. I'm not into that.

Max   Get a fucking *grip*. (*To* **Tadge**.) Let's have a look.

Tadge *passes it to him, his eyes never leaving the blade.* **Max** *feels the weight of it.*

Max   Fuck me. This is army issue? (*Pause.*) That is *nasty*. (*Pause.*) Fits your hand perfectly, doesn't it?

Pause. He passes it to **Alan** *who accepts it awkwardly.*

Somebody was going to *use* that on you?

Tadge *nods, watching the blade.* **Alan** *holds the knife by the handle, getting more used to it.*

Alan   It's *obscene.*

Max   But you have to admit, there's something ... I don't know ...

Alan   Something *what?*

Max   You're telling me it doesn't feel good in your hand?

He passes it back to **Max** *who passes it straight to* **Tadge**. **Alan** *swallows a yelp of dismay.* **Tadge** *looks at the blade, turning it over and over. Pause.*

You *never* had a knife when you were a kid?

Alan   I had a fucking *pen*-knife! With Loch *Lomond* written on the side, yes!

Max   A *pen*-knife.

Alan   Well, I don't know about *you* but I never found myself in the position where I had to skin a fucking *yak*!

He keeps watch on the knife from the corner of his eye. Pause.

I mean, if you really *did* take that knife off someone who was trying to *stab* you with it ... then surely you should *take* it to someone ...

Tadge   Who?

Alan   Well, your ... superior in the army or someone ...

Tadge   But they're all *part* of it!

Alan   Then the *police* ...

Tadge   No they're *everywhere*, not just the *army*, not just the ... the Penetrators, they're every ... you don't *know* ...

A long pause. **Alan** *falls silent.*

Max   But is there any way you can trace a knife like that back to the owner? To prove it's his.

Tadge (*pause*)   No, but it'll have his fingerprints on it.

Pause. They look at the knife and then at each other. Pause.

Max   I think you might have fucked that one up a bit.

Alan   Could we put the knife away now?

Max *and* **Tadge** *look at him.*

Alan   It's just making me a bit nervous.

Tadge (*pause*)   Why?

Alan   It just *does*. Accidents happen round knives.

Pause.

Max   Put it away, Tadge, or we'll never hear the end of it.

Tadge (*pause*)   You think I'm going to hurt you with it?

Alan   It's not *that* . . .

Tadge   No?

Alan   No . . .

Tadge   You don't trust me?

Alan   Yes, I *do*, but . . .

Tadge   You think I'd hurt you with it?

Alan   Not on purpose, no, but . . . (*Pause.*) Look, I'm a bit stoned. Knives – I don't like knives, is that so strange? I *do* live here . . .

Max   Just put it away.

Tadge   You don't *trust* me.

Alan   It's not . . . Look – you're a friend and I don't want to offend you but something's obviously . . . *happened* to you, I don't know what, I don't think *you* know what, and it's obviously freaked you out a bit and I just don't . . . I don't think you should be walking around with something like *that* . . .

Tadge   Why not?

Alan   *Many* reasons – *anything* could happen – kids might get hold of it – someone might use it on *you* even . . .

Tadge   You?

Alan   Not *me*!!

Max (*concerned*)   You're freaking him out, man. It *is* his house too.

Tadge   Maybe you just don't want me to have it.

Alan   I just want you to put it away.

Tadge   Maybe you want to save your pals from the black room, eh?

Alan   What?

Tadge   Your Penetrators.

A long pause. The knife has turned towards **Alan**.

Alan   Just put it away, all right.

Looks at **Max**.

I'm serious, Max. Tell him to put it away or he'll have to leave. Or I will.

Max (*to* **Tadge**)   Stop fucking about, man. Put it away.

Pause. Slowly **Tadge** *goes to put the knife in the bag. He stops mid-action and looks at* **Alan**.

Tadge   I wouldn't hurt you with it. You're my friends. (*Pause.*) Aren't you?

They nod. Pause. **Tadge** *bends down to put the knife back in the bag.*

Alan   I didn't mean you to think . . .

Lightning-fast, **Tadge** *reappears with the knife in his hand, grinning. Both of them get a fright. He starts going into exaggerated poses with* *it, Bruce Lee-style.* **Max** *is amused.* **Alan** *is not.* **Tadge** *is like a thirteen-year-old.*

Alan   Put the fucking thing away, will you??!

Max (*to* **Alan**)   Don't encourage him. He'll stop.

Business from **Tadge***; posing about, spouting lines from films, showing off. Adapt to suit. He sees the teddies and grabs one of them, holding the knife at its throat.* **Max** *finds this amusing.*

Alan   What *is* it everyone's got against *my* fucking *teddies*?!

Tadge (*in funny voice*)   Confess or the teddy gets his head fucked off. Confess.

He grins at **Max***, nodding 'shall I?'* **Max** *laughs, giving teddy the thumbs down.*

Alan (*weary*)   Oh *don't* . . .

Tadge   Then confess. Confess or the teddy bleeds like an Arab. Confess.

Alan *looks plaintively at* **Max**.

Max   You better confess.

Alan   Confess to what?

Tadge   Confess.

Max   Anything.

Alan   I'll confess that I'm a bit *hassled* by this.

Tadge *grins*.

Tadge   You have until five to confess. One. The teddy will die. Confess. Two. Teddy gets it up the arse. Three. Confess.

Alan *looks at* **Max**.

Alan   He better *not*. Really.

Max *shakes his head*.

Tadge   Confess, Penetrator. Four.

He holds teddy up.

Last chance. Last chance to save teddy. Confess.

Alan (*acting bored*)   Please forgive me, teddy, I'm innocent.

Tadge   *Five.*

And with a slight nod of reluctance, he tears the teddy to shreds. It is a vicious and frightening action, all humour going from his face. He finishes, red in the face from effort, and drops the disembowelled teddy on the ground. Pause.

Should have confessed.

Pause. **Max** *and* **Alan** *are gobsmacked.*

Max   What the fuck did you do *that* for?!

Alan *gets up and walks towards the door.*

Alan   That's *it*!

Tadge *points the knife square at* **Alan**'s *chest.* **Alan** *stops, frozen.*

Tadge   Where are you going?

Alan (*pause*)   Let me past.

Tadge   Going to get your friends, eh?

Max   What the *fuck* are you doing?

Tadge (*to* **Max**)   He's not your friend.

Max   What do you mean, he's . . .

Tadge   He was in the black room. I remember him. His voice. The smell of his cock.

Alan *backs off with* **Tadge** *following, knifepoint at his breast.*

Tadge   That's right, Penetrator. You're no friend of mine. You're no friend of Max. You're only friends with your own dirty kind. I know how your kind work, the filth in your head. You want to turn Max against me. You want to tear us apart. Fuck us till we bleed. But he's the brains and I'm the brawn see. One unit. Anti-Penetrator Unit One.

He backs **Alan** *on to the settee.* **Alan** *sits with a thump.* **Tadge**
pins him down, holding the knife to his throat.

Max   Stop this. Stop this now.

Tadge   But you see this? (*Knife.*) Took it off your kind so
I could penetrate the penetrator. Funny eh? Penetrate the
Penetrator. Make you cry like I cried in the black room.
Make you beg like I begged you. Let you feel steel in your
arse. You'd like that, eh? Like me to fuck you like a dog.

Max *approaches him, softly.*

Max   Please. I know you're only kidding. You're not
going to hurt Alan. So stop fucking about.

Tadge   He's not your friend.

Max   He *is*. And I'm *yours* . . .

Tadge   *Are* you?

Max (*pause*)   Of *course* I am!

Tadge   Then why'd you go *away*?!!

Max (*pause*)   *Away*?

Tadge   You went *away*!

Max   From where?

Tadge   From *here*!

Max (*pause*)   I went to college.

Tadge (*mocking*)   'College'!

Max   Look – please – listen to me now. You're ill. You
know you are. Your head's all mixed-up. I'm your friend
and I'm telling you . . .

He leans forwards to **Tadge**'*s arms.*

I'll help you. You'll be good as new sooner then you know.
You don't want to do anything you'll regret . . .

His hands reach **Tadge**'*s wrists, gently close around them.* **Tadge**
smiles, shaking his head.

Tadge   Chinese burns for you, Max. Deadlegs for you.

Max   Give me the knife. You don't want to hurt Alan. Alan's your friend.

Alan *nods fearfully.*

Alan   I am. I'm your friend. I wasn't in the black room I swear.

Tadge (*to* **Max**)   Take your hands off me.

Max (*pause. Raises hands*)   All right. All right. But *think*, man: Alan's your friend. He's *our* friend.

Alan *nods.*

Max   We used to trip together, the three of us, remember? The three wasters, remember? (*Pause.*) Remember that – that time we went camping, and we – we found those mushrooms in that ruin and – and we . . .

Tadge   But what about *us*?! It was *better* before! You were the brains, I was the brawn! We were friends, we were *real* friends, tell me about *that*, tell me what you remember about *that*!

Max *doesn't know what to say.*

Tadge   *Tell* me!

Alan   Tell him.

Max   Tell him what?

Alan   *ANY*-FUCKING-THING!

Tadge   Tell me what you remember!

A long pause.

Max   I remember . . . uh . . . um . . . when your dad . . .

Tadge   HE'S NOT MY *DAD*!

Max   OK OK all right not that . . . Shite Hawkins! Shite Hawkins. Remember him? He bust my lip open and . . . you went and found him by the waste ground . . .

Tadge   And I kicked his *cunt* in for you!

Max   You did . . .

Tadge   I kicked him to *fuck*!

Max   You did. You did. I've never seen anyone get worse.

Tadge   I looked good, didn't I?

Max (*nods*)   You looked good . . .

Tadge   I did, didn't I?

Max   You did. You looked good. I remember. I remember every kick, every punch.

Tadge   No one else ever did that for you!

Max *shakes his head.*

Max   No one. Now please let him go.

A long pause.

Tadge   You don't know what it was like. In the dark. All shrivelled up. Just my hatred keeping me alive. Their hands all over me. And you never came for me. Their dirty cocks in my mouth, up my arse. I know how to kill a man. I'm not afraid. I've seen guys get their ears cut off. I've seen lassies with their cunts shot out. I'm not scared of blood on my hands, hot blood pouring on my hands. Let me out there. Let me do what I do.
(*Sings.*) 'Wounded Arab girl
Lying by the road
I'm so horny I could shoot my load
Fuck her up the arse
Shoot her in the face
But save her cunt for the boys at the base.'

A long pause.

It was better before. Tell me about before. Tell me about the woods.

He slowly drags the knife down over whimpering **Alan***'s chest and* *stomach to his crotch.*

Max   The woods – what *about* the woods?

Tadge   The night we stayed out.

Max   Please – just let him go.

Tadge   Tell me about the woods.

Max (*pause*)   What about them?

Tadge   *One.*

Max   But I don't *remember* . . . !

Tadge   Two.

Alan   Tell him about the fucking *woods*!!!

Max   But what's it got to *do* with anything?!

Tadge   *Three.*

Max   But you *know* what happened, why . . . ?!

Tadge   *Four.*

Alan   For fuck's sake tell him about the fucking woods please tell him about the fucking *woods*!

Max   But . . . !

Tadge   *Fi* . . .

Max   The Woods! The Woods! (*Pause.*) It turned dark on us. We got lost. It was past nine and we couldn't get home . . .

Tadge   We could run better at night, couldn't we?

Max   We could. We said that. We felt lighter. Like we were on strings.

Tadge   We built a bivouac.

Max   That's right. We built a bivouac.

Tadge   You were the brains, eh?

Max (*nods*)   And you were the brawn.

Tadge   It was a good bivouac, eh?

Max (*pause*)   It was a terrible bivouac.

Tadge   It was *good*!

Max   Yes. It was good!

Tadge   You were scared.

Max   So were you. We thought we were going to die. It got really cold.

Tadge   What did we do?

Max (*pause*)   We uh . . . we huddled together. To keep warm.

Tadge   And I said 'Who's your best friend?'

Max (*pause*)   I don't remember . . .

Tadge   I said 'Who's your best *friend*?!'

Max   And I said . . . I said 'You are.'

Tadge   And I said 'Will we always be best friends?'

Max   And I said 'Yes.'

Tadge   Even when we're thirty?

Max   Even when we're thirty.

Tadge   Forty?

Max   Even when we're forty.

Tadge   Fifty sixty seventy eighty?!

Max   Ninety a hundred for ever.

Max *sits down.*

Tadge   And then what happened?

Max *doesn't answer.*

Tadge   What *happened*?!

Max   You *know* what happened.

Tadge   *Tell* me!

Max   You took my trousers down.

Tadge   And then?

Max   My pants.

A long pause.

I lay down on the leaves. (*Pause.*) You pulled my shirt up. You listened to my heart.

Tadge   It was cold.

Max   It was cold, yes.

Tadge   And I touched you.

Max (*nods*)   Yes.

Tadge   Where did I touch you?

Max   You touched my balls. You asked me to cough. You turned me over and spread my arse.

Tadge   Do you remember the smell of me?

Max (*nods*)   Yes.

Tadge   I remember the smell of you.

A long pause. **Tadge** *is calming, the knife slowly coming away from* **Alan**.

And then they came.

Max (*nods*)   And then they came. We saw the torch lights. We heard the leaves, the voices.

A long pause. **Tadge** *slumps back, the knife limp in his hands.*

Tadge   It was better before they came.

Pause. Quickly, **Alan** *grabs the knife from* **Tadge**'*s hand.* **Tadge** *offers no resistance.* **Alan** *gets quickly to the back of the room, holding the knife out threateningly.* **Max** *and* **Tadge** *just sit there.*

Alan   Get him out! Max! Get him out of here! (*Pause.*) Max!

Max *looks at him.*

Max   Put it down, Alan. He wasn't going to hurt you.
He's your friend.

Alan   My – ! I've just been held at fucking *knifepoint* in my
own fucking house by this *psychopath* and you're – !! I mean
who's the fucking *mad* one here??!

Max *leans down and picks up part of the torn teddy. He looks at it,*
stroking its fur with his thumbs.

Alan   He comes here – this *bastard* comes here – spouting
all this shit about Penetrators and Storming Fucking
Norman – he rips my fucking teddy to pieces and then he
sticks a fucking *knife* in my throat whilst I listen to the two
of you recount some *dull commonplace* little *Doctor* game – !
It's fucking *sad* if it wasn't so fucking out*rageous* – I should
have you fucking *done*! I should phone the pigs right *now*!! I
don't *care* about you Tadger fucking *Tadger*! You were a
fucking *bully* then, you're a *bully* now and *you* fucking joined
up and so maybe you got fucked up the arse maybe you
didn't but whatever you get you fucking *deserve*! (*To* **Max**.)
And what are you, just some fucking *henchman* to this *moron*!
Well I want him *out*, I want him out *now* and I *don't* want
to ever see his ugly fucking face again unless he has a
muzzle on him do you fucking *hear* me???!!!

He waves the knife impotently. **Tadge** *doesn't move.* **Max** *stares at*
the teddy-scrap. A long pause.

I'm being *serious*!

Pause. **Max** *looks at him.*

Max   How did you know that Laura set my giraffe on
fire?

A long pause.

Alan   What?

Max   How did you *know* that Laura set my giraffe on fire?

Alan *stares at him, uncomprehending.*

Max   I didn't tell you.

Alan   What has *this* got to do with anything?

Max   I'm just asking you: I didn't tell you. I didn't tell anyone. So how do *you* know?

Alan (*pause*)   *I* don't know. You must have told me.

Max   (*shakes head*)   I didn't tell anyone. Did she tell you?

Alan   I don't know – yes, maybe she did.

Max   She phoned here?

Alan   No – well . . .

Max   Did you see her?

Alan (*pause*)   I must have, I suppose.

Max (*pause*)   Why would you see Laura?

Alan   Why not?

Max   You never did before. You hardly even spoke to her.

Alan   Well – (*Pause.*) Maybe I met her in the street. Yes, I think I did, a couple of weeks ago, yes.

Max   A *couple*?

Alan (*pause. Nods*)   Mmm.

Max   You didn't say.

Alan   Well, I'm not allowed to mention her *name* . . . !

Max (*nods*)   But it was only *last* week that she torched Elmer.

Alan (*pause*)   Then it was . . . yes, right, I got confused, it was *Mary* that I met two weeks ago, yes, sorry . . . Laura I met *last* week um . . . in town . . . yes . . .

A long pause.

Max   This is bullshit, isn't it?

A long pause.

Max   Have you slept with her?

Alan (*pause*)   Max . . .

Max   Just *tell* me: *have* you slept with her?

Alan   Is that all you care about?

Max (*shakes head*)   No. But it's the only difference.

Alan   Between what?

Max   Between friends and lovers.

Alan   Is that what you think? (*Pause.*) I'm not surprised she left you. (*Pause.*) Look at you with your scowl and your speed and your porn mags hidden all over the house. You don't know up from down or old from new. You don't . . .

Max   Get out, Alan. Just go.

Alan (*pause*)   Where can I go?

Max   I don't *give* a fuck. Just go. Go before I . . .

Alan   Before you what? Kick my cunt in?

Max (*pause*)   I wouldn't do that. I'm not that sort of guy.

Alan (*softly*)   No. I know you're not.

Max (*pause*)   But I'd get Tadge to do it.

Wearily, **Tadge** *lifts his head at the mention of his name. A long pause.* **Alan** *drops the knife on the floor and exits. A long pause.*

Tadge   When we were in Germany we had all these videos at the base, right, there was one with these lassies in them that had cunts *and* cocks and they were *real* too and there was one with this guy who could suck his own cock but he had to have like an operation on his back so he could bend over and there was all the usual things but there was one with this girl getting an enemy up her arse and one with these lassies doing *jobbies* honestly and sucking

off pigs' *cocks* and that which are all curly and one where
this lassie sews up her cunt with thread whilst this guy
sticks his *cock* up her arse and that guy had *his* cock up a
... no, he had a cock up his arse and *that* guy, he had a
cock up *his* and this girl's *cunt* who was licking another *cunt*
who was sucking these two *cocks* who each had ...

Max *shifts sickly in his seat.* **Tadge***'s voice fades out until all we
can hear is a stream of murmur, punctuated by obscenities:*

Tadge   Cock
Cunt
cunts
cocks
cock
cock
cunt
cocks
cunts
cocks

And so on until it builds to a crescendo, **Max** *covering his ears and
then:*

Max   Tadge, will you just shut *up*!

Tadge *does, surprised.*

Max   Will you please just ... shut up.

A long pause. **Tadge** *gets up. He wanders into the kitchen. Pause.
He comes out with two packets of Rolos. He kneels down beside*
Max*, handing him some Rolos.* **Max** *looks at them. Pause. He
opens a packet. They sit there eating them.*

Tadge   Your mum used to give us sweets, eh? After tea.

Pause.

I wasn't allowed to have sweets, was I?

They munch on the Rolos. **Tadge***'s foot starts to swing. Softly,
perhaps unconsciously, they start to hum a tune, lost in their own
worlds.*

I used to like coming to your house.

Lights fade on them.

Music.

Notes

Penetrator was a very personal project. Not only was it loosely based on a real-life event, it was written for, and performed by, me and two long-standing friends. As a result, we were able to ad-lib freely and weave many of our own in-jokes into the play. The intimacy and realism of these first scenes made what followed particularly powerful. Anyone performing this play should seek to create a similar atmosphere. These notes indicate the intention behind certain moments so that you may feel to change them as you see fit.

1. Here, Alan is doing an impression of Bruce Forsyth, a British game-show host who has the habit of repeating the last words of people's sentences. There's no particular point to this other than to establish familiarity. As for the contents of the shopping bag, adapt to suit.
2. This play was written not long after the Gulf War. This element is not as important as it might appear, mainly lending some topicality. You could choose to keep it as it is and treat the play as period, or you could substitute another item of topical news, preferably a similar conflict. Failing that, you might find that all references can be lost.
3. This next section mentions various television shows from the characters' childhood. Again, adapt to suit but bear in mind that disillusionment with childhood is a theme of the play, especially in Max's case.
4. Creamola Foam was the kind of gassy chemical drink that only kids like.
5. At the time, late-night television seemed to show badly dubbed Alain Delon movies every couple of nights.
6. All the odd names mentioned here are characters from children's television shows – a bunch of puppet firemen. Hambel was a grotesque doll from an infants' programme called *Play School*.
7. Various coarse Scottishisms concerning the male genitals. It's a general rule that when Max and Alan (but not Tadge) are being vulgar, they adopt funny voices as a distancing technique.

8. Reference to a particularly naive anti-war song by Culture Club.

9. Again, as this play is not really about the army, it's not *absolutely* vital that Tadge's imaginary father is a military man, just that he's a public figure. However, it makes more thematic sense that he is.

10. Here, Max can say whatever he likes, as he's simply trying (unsuccessfully) to diffuse the tension. You might want to leave this open so as to react to topical events. Return to text when Tadge speaks.

'The Knife Sequence': It's virtually impossible to script this scene, so what you have here is only a guideline. The scene is designed to be played at the highest pitch of intensity and you should bear in mind that it will take a long time to reach that pitch. It's far and away the most draining sequence I've ever seen played on stage but – if it's done right – uniquely shattering. Good luck to you.

Year of the Family

Year of the Family was first performed at the Finborough Theatre, London, on 28 March 1994 (European Year of the Family). The cast was as follows:

Sid	Alastair Galbraith
Claire	Sophie Langham
Dickie	Roger McKern
Fliss	Rachel Weisz
Tramp	Timothy Barlow

Directed by Anthony Neilson
Designed by Michael T. Roberts
Sound by Neil Alexander

Characters

Sid
Claire
Dickie
Fliss
Tramp

Act One

One

Music.

This is an exact foreshadowing of Scene Twenty-Seven played identically but without dialogue.

*As far as the audience are concerned we are watching a Christmas party scene – a young girl (**Fliss**) miming, another girl (**Claire**) and an older man ('**Henry**') trying to guess. A young man (**Sid**) sits drunkenly in a chair, watching. They all wear party hats. The game over, **Fliss** approaches the old man, says something to him. He is intrigued and surprised.*

They turn to us expectantly, waiting for someone's arrival.

Lights fade.

Two

Night.

Sid *crouches at the window – a camera with a telephoto lens sits on a tripod. He's watching something across the road.*

Claire, *nearby, is feeling her left breast through her shirt, in what seems at first to be an absently sexual manner, but her face takes a concerned expression and the caress is revealed as an examination.*

Claire It's back.

Pause. **Sid** *is preoccupied.*

Did you hear me? It's come back.

Sid It's nothing.

Claire It's my breast. I should know.

Sid I've told you – cancerous growths don't shoot around

your body like fucking pinballs. It's what he said: a gland.
Nothing.

Claire   It *feels* like something.

A long pause.

Maybe he's not in.

Sid   He's in.

Pause.

Claire   We could go for a bop. I fancy a bop. (*Pause.*) It's
Saturday night.

Sid   Chicken.

Claire   I'm not a chicken.

Sid   Prude.

Claire   I'm *not* a prude.

Sid   Virgin Mary, is it?

Claire   No.

Sid   *No.*

Pause.

Claire   I just fancy a bop. It's Saturday night. That's
what people do on Saturday night.

Sid   Is *that* what they do?

Claire   Boyfriends. Girlfriends.

Sid   Right. Like you and old saggy balls. Disco Inferno.

He becomes animated.

Yes! There he is!

*He turns the lamp off, crouching there in the orange glow of the
streetlamp, watching through the viewfinder.*

Come and see.

Pause. She wanders over to him, mock-casual. He pulls her down, lets her look. Pause, and then she inhales sharply.

Claire   Oh my God!

She giggles, shocked.

What's he *doing*?!

Sid *puts on a stupid expression.*

Claire   I *know* – but walking *around* like that?

Pause.

What's he doing *now*?!

Sid *pushes her aside. Pause.*

Sid   He's hanging a *shirt* off it! (*Laughs.*) Ya fuckin' beauty!!

Claire   Why's he *doing* that?

Sid (*shrugs*)   Maybe there's no space in the airing cupboard.

Her turn again. She shifts the camera slightly.

Claire   Look, there's some people having dinner . . .

Sid *shifts the camera back, forcing her to look.*

Sid   How old would you say he is? Sixteen?

Claire (*pause*)   Bit older.

Sid   Not bad for his age though, eh? What d'you reckon? Bigger than me?

Claire   I'm not close enough. (*Pause.*) Yours is very big.

Sid   Don't fucking *humour* me.

She stops looking, stands up.

Claire   What's the time?

Sid   Why? (*Sarcastic.*) Got to get back?

Claire (*sighs*)   *No.* Maybe we could catch the late show at the cinema.

Sid Mary Whitehouse, is it?

Claire It's Saturday *night*.

Sid That doesn't turn you on?

Pause. She says nothing. He turns the lamp on again, and **Claire** *ducks down.*

Claire *Sid*!

Pause. She shakes her head. He smiles wickedly. His smile infects her.

Sid Stand up.

Claire He'll *see* me!

Sid That's the *point*.

Pause.

Claire Why?

Sid Because I want you to.

Pause. And then, tentatively, she stands. **Sid** *jumps up and waves frantically across the street, shouting. She ducks again, laughing.*

Claire You fucking *bastard*!!

Sid Stand *up*.

Claire He's looking over!

Pause. He leans forward and kisses her deeply. Pause. She stands. Pause.

Sid What's he doing?

Claire He's looking at me. (*Pause.*) Oh God. He's waving at me.

Sid What with?

His hand creeps up her skirt. She shudders. Pause. She nods. Her hand touches his shoulder.

Don't tell me it doesn't turn you on. You like a big cock. Maybe it doesn't matter inside, but to look at – to anticipate – to be *desired* – it gets the juices flowing, doesn't it? Yes. Pussy doesn't lie.

His hand moving under her skirt. Her fingers in his hair. **Sid** *moves her hand to her breast. She drops it away. He moves it back again.*

Go on. Give the boy a thrill. Give the boy a thrill and he'll think about you all his life. He'll think about you before he sleeps. He'll think about you on his wedding night. Be a dirty girl. Be a dirty girl for him and he'll think of you when he dies.

She fondles her breasts, losing herself. **Sid** *pushes his free hand down his trousers, starts to masturbate. She looks down at him.*

Claire   Sid – let's make love.

But he just continues what he's doing. Music for a while over this until the lights fade.

Three

Claire *is sitting at a table in a posh café. Cappuccino in front of her. This is not her natural habitat.*

A while, and then **Dickie***, a middle-aged man, comes in. We can see her expression freeze over as he approaches. He just stands there.*

Claire   What are you doing here?

Dickie   I'm on my break. (*Pause.*) I knew you were meeting Fliss so –

Pause.

Claire   So are you just going to stand there?

Pause. **Dickie** *sits down. Awkwardness.*

Look, I was at Jennie's, all right?

Dickie   I didn't say anything.

Claire   You don't *have* to, do you?

Pause.

There's nothing wrong if I want to stay at a friend's house. I'm only twenty-fucking-*one*, you know?

Dickie   I'm very aware of that.

Pause.

I just wanted to see you.

Claire   Well, you've *seen* me.

Long pause.

How's work?

Dickie   Computers crashed, but apart from that . . . (*Pause.*) Thought you were at college today?

She shakes her head. Pause.

Maybe we could go out tonight. Go to the pictures.

Pause. She nods.

You could meet me after work.

Claire   I'd rather not.

Dickie   Why not?

Claire   You know why not.

Dickie   Claire, it's been a long time now. Nobody's bothered.

Claire   I am.

Pause. He reaches out to touch her hand. She jumps as if shocked. Pause.

Dickie   What's wrong, Claire?

Pause.

Claire   There's nothing wrong. Not with you.

He smiles without humour.

What?

Dickie *shakes his head. A moment, and then* **Fliss** *enters, a blur of hyperactivity, beautiful and expensively dressed.*

Fliss Claire – I'm so sorry – the tubes are just from *hell* today!

She sees **Dickie**.

Claire Dickie, this is Fliss. Felicity – Richard.

They shake hands.

Fliss We meet at last. She likes to keep her men hidden away, my little sister. Now I can see why.

Pause. **Dickie** *looks at* **Claire**. **Fliss**'*s hand goes to her mouth.*

No, no, no, that came out all wrong! (*To* **Claire**.) That's always happening to me, isn't it? I pay someone a compliment and it comes out all *wrong*! It *was* a compliment, I swear! Oh Fliss, your silly mouth!

She smacks her own hand, smiling broadly. Pause.

Dickie Anyway – I should be getting back . . .

Fliss *exclaims in disappointment.* **Dickie** *nods.*

Dickie Back to the grind.

Fliss And where's that?

Dickie Newman House. (*Pause.*) Social Security.

Fliss Oh how depressing. All those desperate people. (*Pause.*) Of course, that's where you met Claire, isn't it?

Pause. **Dickie** *nods, a smile passing between him and* **Claire**.

Dickie Anyway, nice to meet you. (*To* **Claire**.) You'll be home later?

Claire *nods. He starts to leave, but* **Claire** *stops him. She kisses him, for* **Fliss**'*s benefit. Pause. He leaves.* **Fliss** *and* **Claire** *sit down.*

Fliss *Well.*

Claire Well what?

Fliss You didn't tell me he was . . . so much *older*. I mean comparatively. Not that he isn't attractive. (*Pause.*) How old *is* he?

Claire Fliss – I didn't come here for the joy of your company. Just tell me what you wanted to tell me.

Pause. **Fliss** *is hurt.*

Fliss I don't understand what I've done to you, Claire – that you should hate me so much –

Claire (*sighs*) I don't *hate* you –

Fliss (*tearful*) All I've ever wanted is for us to be a family – God knows, after all that's happened I could –

She dabs at her eyes with a serviette.

And I suppose you've told him.

Claire (*pause*) No.

Fliss You *have*! You *have* told him!

Claire I haven't.

Fliss Why did you pause before you said no, then? You always pause before you lie, you always do!

Claire This is why I don't call you, Fliss. Talking to you's a waste of breath.

Pause.

Fliss I want some coffee.

Claire *pushes hers over to* **Fliss**. *Pause.*

Fliss Why don't you have a bite to eat? You don't eat enough.

Claire *Fliss* –

Fliss Well, Claire, this is important news, it can't just be *blurted* out! (*Pause.*) I don't even know why I'm telling you, I know what you'll say.

Pause. **Fliss** *collects herself, then takes* **Claire***'s reluctant hand.*

I've found him.

Long pause, **Claire** *just staring at her.*

(*Nods.*) I know. I can barely believe it myself. All these years I thought I had faith, but it was only when I saw him that I realised that I'd all but lost hope. But I didn't jump to conclusions. I watched him for weeks, circling closer and closer until there was no doubt in my mind.

Tearful, she grips **Claire***'s hand.*

No doubt this time, Claire. No doubt.

Pause. **Claire** *pulls her hand away, rises to leave.*

Claire   You are *cracked*. You know that? Seriously.

Fliss   Claire, please don't go –

She grabs onto **Claire***'s jacket.* **Claire** *pulls away, trying to keep her voice down:*

Claire   He's *dead*! Get it through your stupid head! He's been dead over twenty fucking *years*!

Fliss *shakes her head, smiling.*

Fliss   He's come back to us.

Claire   To *you*. He's nothing to do with me, remember?!

Fliss   Why don't you wait until you see him before you –?

Claire   I am not getting sucked into your sick fantasies!

Fliss   I need you to help me –

Claire   No.

Fliss   Please.

Claire   Why should I?!

Fliss   Because you're my *sister* – !

Claire   Only half.

Fliss   We're still connected by blood! (*Pause.*) I help you: whenever you've needed money I've given it to you, haven't I? You can't say I haven't! And now I'm asking you to help *me*!

Pause. **Claire** *sighs.*

Claire   What kind of help?

Fliss (*pause*)   Help with mummy.

Pause. **Claire** *shakes her head, at a loss.*

Claire   You're incredible, you know that? I mean you are just – so fucking *mad*!

And with this, **Claire** *leaves. Pause.* **Fliss** *is suddenly aware of everyone looking. Innocently, she sniffs the artificial rose on the table, and then realises her mistake.*

Lights fade.

Four

Fliss *enters her flat. She looks behind her, then exits. When she reappears she is leading a tramp into her living-room, as one might lead a wary child. The* **Tramp**, *in his late forties at least, looks barely human, swaddled in cast-offs. His face is a map of blood vessels, his nose like a sponge. A heavy beard. The soft white of* **Fliss**'s *hand is incongruous in his leathery palm.*

Fliss   It's all right. You're safe.

Once in, she gently lets go of his hand. He stands there looking around.

I know it's small but it was the best deal I could get on a two-bedroom place. (*Pause.*) It's nice in the summer. The sun comes up on the bedroom side and moves round here in the afternoon. I think that's important, don't you? I do a bit of writing myself. Just little things, poems, my diary. Nothing to show. But it's nice for that. (*Pause.*) I mean it'll do until we get back on our feet. (*Pause.*) It's better than a bloody bench!

She's got annoyed. She calms, softens.

Why don't you take your coat off?

Pause. She goes to help him off with his coat, he pulls away. Pause. He allows her to continue. She takes his coat off, but there is another underneath. Coat after coat. None of them smell too good. Eventually the rather scrawny man at their heart is revealed. She takes the coats and throws them out of the window. He watches this blankly.

She exits. We hear the sound of water running into a bath. The **Tramp** *wanders over to the window and looks out at his clothes.* **Fliss** *reappears, carrying new clothes over her arm.*

Fliss   Now there's scissors and a razor in there . . . some shaving gel too, the expensive stuff. (*Pause.*) And then there's this.

She holds the suit up for him to see. It is beautifully made, perhaps tweed.

It's yours. Do you remember it?

Pause. He reaches out to touch the material, fingertips at first but then feeling its quality between his fingers. He stoops to smell it, breathing it in. He looks at her. She stares at him, entranced.

You don't even know who I am. Do you? (*Pause.*) I'll make you some coffee. You can have it in your bath. (*Pause.*) Not *in* your bath – you know what I mean.

She drapes the suit over his arm and leaves him standing there. He strokes the suit. Then we hear the sound of screeching brakes, faint at first but building, building, repeating and building. The **Tramp** *hears it, frightened, his hands going to his ears as the screeching builds to a terrible impact. A metal-rending crash.*

Lights out.

Five

Claire *sits blindfolded, waiting.*

Dickie *appears behind her wearing the most god-awful casual jacket and panama hat.*

Dickie   OK. You can look now.

Hesitantly she takes the blindfold off.

The new Dickie!

She just stares at him. Unreadable.

What d'you think? (*Pause.*) Jacket's not bad is it? And guess how much. (*Pause.*) Guess.

Claire (*pause*)   Eighty pounds?

Dickie (*pause*)   Eighty? You're out of step. You don't get a jacket like this for eighty pounds, not these days. All the young lads are wearing them and they won't spend less than a hundred, or it's not credible. (*Pause.*) No, it was one twenty. But it's a good thick jacket. It'll last me. (*Pause.*) Anyway I need something a bit more practical. Casual but practical. (*Pause.*) And I've always fancied a hat, I just never had the guts to wear one but then I thought 'What the hell', you know. (*Pause.*) You're only as young as you feel.

She just stares at him.

(*Pause.*) Maybe it's a bit over-the-top. (*Pause.*) I can always take it back. (*Pause.*) But I thought it went quite nicely with the jacket. (*Pause.*) Maybe it *would* be better, something more discreet. I don't know. (*Pause.*) I've never been much on fashion. Lara always did that. (*Pause.*) I just thought I'd push the boat out. (*Pause.*) I mean they can always be taken back. (*Pause.*) There were some other jackets that were nice, but they were a little more expensive.

Claire *nods. He is getting smaller and smaller.*

Dickie   Well, I can always wear them for a couple of days. See how I feel. (*Pause.*) I was just a bit bored with myself. Feeling a bit fuddy-duddy.

He puts his hand in his pocket.

Hey, there's something in the pocket here.

He fishes inside it and brings out a wrapped present.

What's this? It says something on it. (*Pause.*) It says – 'For Claire'.

Smiling, he hands it to her. She accepts it.

That must be you.

She unwraps the package. It's a tape. She sighs.

Claire   Oh, Dickie ...

Dickie   I've heard you humming along with it. (*Pause.*) There was another one I was thinking of, but I thought you might have it already. (*Pause.*) You don't have that one, do you?

Pause. She looks at him sheepishly.

(*Pause.*) You *do*?

Pause. She nods.

Dickie (*pause*)   Well, that's no problem. The receipt's in there. You can just swap it for something else. (*Pause.*) Or I can do it.

A long pause.

Oh well.

Claire   I'm sorry.

Dickie   It's not *your* fault. (*Pause.*) It's no problem.

Pause. He takes his jacket off. Pause.

Better go and hang this up.

She nods. He exits. She sits there. Clouds pass over the sun. She sighs heavily. He comes back in.

Can I see?

She passes him the tape. He sits down, reading the track listing. She watches him. He finishes. Pause.

How did it go with your sister?

Claire *groans holding her head.*

Dickie   She seemed nice.

Claire   You mean you fancy her.

Dickie   *No* . . . I mean she seems nice.

Claire   You've got no idea whether she's nice or not.

Dickie   I just said she *seemed* . . .

Claire   She's not any nicer than anyone else. She *seems* a lot of things, but it's all put on . . . the posh voice, the little girl lost look. *And* she's a bloody Tory.

He smiles. She looks at him.

What's funny?

Dickie   Well – (*Pause.*) I just detect a hint of sibling rivalry.

Claire   *Rivalry?* Why would I want to . . . *rival* her? I'm not joking when I say she's mad. She's a fucking nutter.

Dickie   In what way?

Claire   In *every* way.

Dickie   You know, in all this time, you've never told me anything about your family.

Claire   You've never told me anything about *yours*.

Dickie   What d'you want to know?

Claire   I don't want to know *anything*!

Dickie   Then how is she mad?

Claire (*sighs*)   I don't want to go into it.

Dickie (*pause*)   Do you mean actually *mad* or do you mean that she's a bit eccentric?

Claire   What do you mean eccentric?

Dickie   Well, you can't stand on a plug-hole. That's eccentric.

Claire   Well, you eat raw *bacon*.

Dickie   No, that's a *preference*. (*Smiles.*) You can't breathe in when your belly-button's covered.

Claire   Well, I *can't*. (*Pause.*) You write lists.

Dickie   You pretend you don't fart.

Claire (*laughs*)   I *don't*!

Dickie   You sleep with a little cushion.

Claire   You get depressed by *feet*. *And* hot baths. *And* you keep your dog's ashes in a box!

Dickie   You're scared of worms and pigeons and you're scared of the dark.

Claire   And you're scared of wasps. And silence. And being naked.

Dickie   That's just consideration for others.

He is over by her now. He touches the side of her face. We can see her freeze. He stares lovingly at her. Pause.

Claire   What?

Dickie (*pause*)   You're very beautiful, Claire.

Pause. She looks away.

Don't you believe me?

Claire (*pause*)   I believe you think I am.

She says nothing. He goes to kiss her and she gives him only her cheek. He kisses her neck, desperately. She remains detached. He turns her round putting her hand on his crotch. She undoes his flies and reaches in, tugging at his dick. He rests his head on her shoulder. She keeps her face turned away. She wants it over with. He gums at her ear, her eyes shut painfully. He whispers to her and his words cut her. He whispers her name over and over until he comes.

Six

Fliss's *apartment.*

A table set for one. Knife and fork, spoon, napkin. A candle burns there. A bottle of wine and two glasses. Too hot from the kitchen **Fliss** *takes off her top. She is wearing a slip underneath.*

Behind her the **Tramp** *enters. He is clean-shaven now, almost glowing. He wears the tweed suit.* **Fliss** *sees him. She just stands there staring at him for a while, her eyes misting over. She wants to say something, yet cannot. Then she just goes to him, hugging him tight, her head against his chest. He barely responds, just looks down at the top of her head. He breathes in the smell of her hair.*

Fliss (*tearful*) It's like it was all a dream. Like it was all just some terrible dream.

A long pause. She collects herself, stands back from him.

Look at you. So handsome.

The **Tramp**'s *hand goes to his beard but it isn't there any more. Pause.* **Fliss** *leads him over to the table.*

Fliss Now you sit here. I've got your favourite for you. Back in a sec.

She exits hurriedly. Pause. He picks up the bottle of wine and slugs back nearly half of it. He places it back as she reappears, carrying a steaming plate of food. She places it in front of him.

(*Smiles.*) Pommes de terre. Petits pois. Steak.

He just stares at it.

You want me to cut it up for you?

Pause. He looks at her with the hint of a scowl. He picks up his knife and fork and goes to cut his steak. He slices off a piece and eats it as she watches.

It should be tender. It was expensive enough. Not that I

really ever have steak. I'm mostly vegetarian, though I'm
not one of those right-on types. I'm not a feminist or
anything. (*Pause.*) Well, no I *am* in some ways, I *used* to be.
I'm sort of a *lapsed* feminist, I suppose.

*He stops eating. A puzzled look on his face. He reaches inside his
mouth.*

What's wrong?

*He rummages about for a while. And then produces something from
his mouth. It's a tooth. He shows it to* **Fliss**.

Is that a *tooth*? (*Pause.*) Is it *yours*? (*Pause.*) That's *terrible*. It
said it was *tender*. It said on the packet it was tender!

She gets up, flustered. She lifts the plate.

Don't eat it then, it said it was tender. I'll get you
something else.

He gently reaches for the plate.

No, no. I'll fix something else. Honestly. I thought it would
be . . . tender.

*She pulls the plate away, tearfully, goes briskly to the window and
scrapes the food off. The* **Tramp** *is half up.* **Fliss** *stomps back to
the table where she sits hard down and pours herself a glass of wine
from the half-empty bottle. The* **Tramp** *is at the window now,
staring out forlornly.*

Fliss   It's all turning into a *fiasco*!

*She is upset. He walks over to her. She looks up at him. Pause. And
then she hugs him again. Her head against his belly.*

I don't know what do to.
I don't know what to say.
It all turns out wrong.

*He strokes her head with his trembling hand. Tentatively, he reaches
for the bottle of wine. Gently, she stops his hand.*

You don't remember anything, do you?

She breaks away from him.

When I first saw you you were standing in the road, screaming at the cars. Why were you doing that? You were angry with them. Did a car hurt you? Were you hurt by a car?

He stares at her, silent.

Do you remember a crash? Being in a crash?

His eyes flicker with the tiniest spark of recognition.

When we lived in Bangor – in Wales – you were working at the university, do you remember that? You were driving home along the country road and you hit another car and there was an explosion, an explosion and flames – do you remember? Flames?

They thought you died. Everyone thought you were dead – *I* thought you were dead! There were three bodies all burnt up so we just assumed one of them was you – we didn't think of other possibilities – nobody thought there might have been another man –

He looks at her, startled.

Do you remember? A hitch-hiker maybe? Did you pick up a hitch-hiker? Or maybe he was in trouble – or hurt? Try to remember: a man, big like you, he went missing from a nearby village just a few nights before. They thought he was you, but you must have got away –

Pause.

There was a bag in the car full of stuff that didn't belong to you, a pair of shoes but not in your size – did it belong to the man?

He sits, his eyes full of horror.

I told them. But they had their quota of bodies. Everything neat and tidy. Everything so convenient, except for me. 'But what proof do you have? Where's the evidence?' But you know, don't you? You know when someone you love is dead. You feel it, in here. (*Pause.*) Do you understand what I'm telling you?

She kneels beside him, taking his hands.

I'm your *daughter*. Fliss. Felicity.

A long pause. He looks at her.

(Nods, smiling.) And this place is yours, as much as it's mine. I bought it with the money you left me and some that I earned. I haven't just sat around doing nothing.

Slowly he reaches out and touches the side of her face. She pushes against his hand like a cat.

I know. I feel the same. So many years stolen away. Years we should've had. How do we have it back? How do we fill that space? How do we fill the blackness? *(Pause.)* But I'll fill it for you, Daddy. I'll give you back your life.

Seven

Claire *is putting her make-up on.*

Claire   Is this a violent thing?

There is no reply.

I don't know if I want to see some thing violent. *(Pause.)* Isn't there something lighter on? A comedy? Or something romantic?

Sid *enters.*

Sid   This *is* romantic.

Claire *(pause)*   It doesn't *sound* romantic. It sounds violent. *(Pause.)* Something like *Breakfast at Tiffany's* that's what I fancy.

Sid   We can stay in if you prefer.

Claire *(pause)*   No, we'll go. I just thought there might be something more . . . you know . . .

Sid   Send them home with a smile?

Claire   Well why not?

Sid   Good clean family fun?

Claire   It doesn't have to be *clean.*

Sid   We could go to a porno then. That's romantic. Swedish Nuns Suck Cock For Jesus, something like that. I could finger-fuck you in the back row.

He is kneeling beside her now, watching her apply her make-up. She stops, looks at him.

Claire   Is this lipstick all right?

Sid   What happened to the really red one?

Claire (*pause*)   That one? Did you like that one? (*Pause.*) I thought it was a bit tacky.

Sid   You suit tacky.

Claire   Thanks.

Sid   Makes your mouth look more like a cunt.

Claire   Maybe I should grow a beard as well.

Sid   I thought you'd started.

She smiles sarcastically.

Give us a kiss.

Pause. She kisses him lightly.

Properly.

Pause. She kisses him on the lips. Eventually she draws away, smiling.

Claire   Lips taste funny.

Sid   Do they?

Her lips start to burn. He watches her.

What is it?

Claire (*pause*)   My lips have gone all hot. What have you been eating?

He says nothing.

Claire Oh, Sid, they're really burning! What have you got on your lips?

He shows her a small bottle of Tabasco sauce, smiling. She rubs at her lips.

That's really nasty.

Sid No. That's romantic. My kiss burns your lips.

Claire You're a bastard, Sid.

Sid I thought you liked Tabasco.

She gets up and goes for a glass of water.

You should try kissing a girl who's wearing loads of perfume. When I was a kid, I used to get off with these girls at parties. You'd be kissing their necks for hours and I swear, by the end of it you'd feel like you'd drunk half a bottle of Charlie, or whatever it was. Used to give me stomach-ache like fuck. And your balls would be aching because your dick had been up and down a dozen times.

Claire *comes back in. Sits down. Sulking. Long pause.*

Claire That was a really nasty thing to do.

Sid Wait a minute . . . we're going to go out tonight. We're probably going to come back here, we'll *probably* end up fucking, and then you'll leave and go home to fuck some sad old man who's been waiting for you all night, and you're saying that *I'm* nasty?

A long pause.

Claire I'm not going to be fucking him.

Sid Even nastier.

Claire What happens if I leave him? Would you be with me?

Sid Who is it that you love?

Claire (*pause*) I love you both in different ways.

Sid Bollocks.

He pulls her, still on the chair, over to him.

Let me rephrase the question: Who is it that you want to fuck?

She doesn't answer, slightly frightened by him.

Come on, don't be shy. Firm and fertile testicles rolling smoothly against your twat, or big saggy balls slapping the backs of your knees? A stiff five-hour Rolls-Royce fuck or half an hour in a stalling Trabant?

Claire Well as far as you're concerned I'm still waiting on the *bus*.

Sid You *blame* me? You think I'm going to fuck you after him? It'd be like going second on a fucking johnny! (*Pause.*) And how's it going to be in twenty years, eh? Or do you reckon force-feeding someone mashed-up rusks could be incorporated into foreplay? After the emptying of the colostomy bag, but just before removing the hernia briefs?

Claire Please, Sid. (*Pause.*) Don't.

Sid Or maybe in ten years' time, when that peachy skin isn't snapping back like it once did and your thighs are getting that waterbed look about them and your womb's dropped and your hour-glass figure is more like a German beer tankard – hey! Along comes another little baby-doll looking for daddy, and sooner than you can say mid-life crisis you've been dumped on your sweet, spreading arse. Why not? He did it to his wife, why wouldn't he do it to you?

A long pause.

Claire You've got a vicious tongue.

Pause. He stares at her then splashes some Tabasco onto his fingers and rubs it into his lips. Pause.

Sid   Kiss me. (*Pause.*) My lips are burning too. Kiss me.

Pause. She kisses him a long time till they break.

See? I don't care. You want to piss on me? You want to shit on me? I don't care.

He splashes more Tabasco on his fingers and puts his hand up her skirt.

Claire   Don't, Sid . . .

Sid   No, come on. You've got to get into it. You like Tabasco.

Claire   On steak, yeah.

Sid   But it's just a twist, isn't it? You just say: this is not pain, this is pleasure. You told me how when you were a kid and you had a loose tooth, you would push it hard into your gum, as hard as you could. It's just the same, that tiny, sweet pain.

She winces as the pain comes. She grips his collar.

That's right. We're the same, you and me. We want to burn. We can burn together.

She grabs a handful of his hair. He speaks through his own pain.

We can have a couple of kids, a dog, a house, and burn them too. Back to fucking basics. Why do you think they call it a nuclear family? Because they're burning alive. Because they burn and everything burns with them, till there's nothing for miles. What will the neighbours say? Fuck all, because they're burning too, all of them, behind their net curtains, the blue rinses burning, the Union Jack burning, burning in the schools, burning in the jumble sales. Burn the right brick and the whole house burns and then the street and then the cities, crumbling black fucking tinder box music box music hall burning churches burning pigs children burning like their fathers burnt and their fathers before them and their fathers before them the whole thing burning down.

Eight

Two scenes play at once, music playing throughout:

*First, **Dickie**, who is simply waiting for **Claire** to come home. He looks out the window. He sits in his chair. He looks at his watch.*

*Simultaneously, we see **Fliss** kissing the **Tramp** good night. She shows him where the bedroom is and then leaves him standing there. Eventually he exits. He is gone a long time. And then he reappears carrying a quilt and a pillow. He sets them down on the floor and lies on top of them. Pause. And then he removes the pillow. Only then can he sleep.*

Dickie *too has drifted off. The moon is full.*

Nine

*The sound of screeching brakes builds to a terrible impact and the **Tramp** wakes. It is daylight now and it takes him a moment or two to reorientate himself. He sits up. Beside him is an envelope. He picks it up, looks at it and discards it again. He gets up and goes to the door. It is locked. He tries the window but it too is locked. There is just him and the envelope. Pause. He pulls out the letter. The paper is slightly yellowed and fragile. We hear it read, probably in **Fliss**'s voice:*

March 16th 1967

Dear Henry,

It's after midnight as I write this, and I'm at my desk looking out the cloudless sky. It's a warm feeling to think that – even though we are so many miles apart – we both look up at the same cathedral of stars and the same bright moon.

I know you'd say that I *am* a child, but I've certainly felt like one recently. But then isn't that what we love? Every morning like Christmas morning, the world a new shape, each sense jangling like a cat's in summer. It's embarrassing how much joy I get from seeing your name written down or from saying it aloud. I even find myself twisting conversations so I can get it in. Oh, and if you're wondering where your gloves are you left them here. Don't worry, they're safe – in fact I keep them under my pillow. Floopy feels quite left out!

I hope you don't think I'm getting all heavy on you. Of course I'd be really happy if you wanted to see me again, but even if you didn't I'd still be glad that I met you and that we did what we did. I have never felt so easy with someone as I did with you, and I'm sure we can be friends. Although I'd prefer to be *more* than friends! Anyway, I have to say bye-bye now before I make a fool of myself. I'll start and end the days thinking of you. Write if you've got the time.

Lots and lots of squelchy kisses, Janis.

PS Have you heard the new Dylan album? It's quite different. I think you'd like it.

Pause. He feels the texture of the paper, smells it. We hear the door unlocking, and **Fliss** *comes in. She stands there, watching him – he is sat with the letter in his hand. Pause.*

Fliss (*pause*)   Did you read it?

Pause. He nods.

Does it mean anything to you?

Pause. He looks at the letter.

You're Henry. Henry is you. That's your name, Henry Gaines.

She indicates herself.

Felicity Gaines. And the letter's from Janis Gaines – well, she wasn't Janis Gaines then but she would be. Your wife. My mother. That was her first ever letter to you. You were thirty-five. She was twenty-three, at college in Manchester, doing History and English Literature. You were up there teaching – Greek History, I think it was – that was when you met. Don't know if it was very ethical. But then it was the sixties.

Pause. She crosses to a small chest, which she opens. From it she produces a small bundle of letters, tied with ribbons. Pause. He reaches for them but she doesn't give them to him.

No. We can't rush this. God knows, I'm as eager as you but we have to be patient – build you up, brick by brick. Trust me I know. (*Pause.*) It's weird, isn't it? This is all that's left of you: a few books, some clothes, what's in my head. And these letters.

She takes one out of the bundle and holds it up. He reaches for it and again she withholds it.

I know, you must be burning to read more. I would be too. But it's so easy to be traumatised, to get scared. And then one day you'd just up and run away. It'd be all too much for you and you'd go. (*Pause.*) I don't know what I'd do if I lost you again. I really don't.

Pause. She gazes at him.

Will you hold me?

Pause. She lifts his arms around her. Awkwardly, he holds her. She snuggles contentedly against him. He reaches for the letter. She kisses him, his neck. Something too intimate about it.

Give me a kiss.

Pause. He kisses her forehead, briefly. He smells her hair.

Properly.

She indicates her lips. Pause. He kisses her there, too long and she breaks away smiling. He has gentle hold of the letter between thumb and forefinger. She won't let go.

Tramp Please.

Pause. She sits up, surprised. They stare into each other's eyes. She lets the letter go.

Lights fade.

Ten

Dickie *and* **Claire** *sit together at the breakfast table. They are both silent.* **Claire** *has a mug of coffee.* **Dickie** *drinks tea, eats toast. The atmosphere is thick with grievance.* **Claire** *can hear each slurp of tea, each crunch of toast. She can hear them travelling down his throat and swilling around his teeth. She can hear each rattle of breath and it's driving her to distraction.*

Dickie   Got college today?

Claire (*nods*)   But I don't think I'll go.

Dickie (*nods*)   Yes, you must be tired.

He drinks more tea. Slurp, slurp, slurp. Toast being chewed. **Claire** *shifts in her seat. He butters some more. The sound of the knife scraping the bread. The clank of metal on plate. Pause.*

So how do you know Jenny?

Claire   Jenny?

Dickie   Yes, Jenny. You just spent the night with her, remember?

Claire   Oh – yes – sorry I'm a bit . . . (*Pause.*) She's an old friend from school.

Dickie   How long's she back for?

Claire (*pause*)   Just a few days.

Pause. He nods. Slurp slurp. Chew chew, Scrape, scrape. This goes on until **Claire** *can bear it no longer.*

Look – Dickie –

Pause. He looks at her.

We should talk.

A long pause.

Dickie   Should we?

His heart is pounding. She nods.

What about?

Claire (*pause*)   Things.

Dickie (*nods*)   Things.

Claire (*sighs*)   I've been doing some . . .

Dickie   I don't mind.

Claire (*pause*)   What?

Dickie   You seeing your friends. I just wish you'd call. (*Pause.*) Sometimes I worry that's all. It's not safe out there.

Claire (*pause*)   That's not what I mean.

Dickie   No, but we don't have to talk about that.

Claire   No.

Dickie   I know you have to see your friends.

Pause. She nods.

Claire   But we should talk anyway.

Pause.

Dickie   Oh. Right. (*Pause.*) Yes. (*Pause.*) Talk then.

A very long pause.

Claire   Well, I can't just . . . (*Pause.*) I think . . .

Dickie *looks at his watch.*

Dickie   Is it something important?

Claire   Well – yes . . . (*Pause.*) Sort of.

Dickie   Because I have to go to work. (*Pause.*) In fact I'm already late.

Claire   It's not something I can just . . . say. (*Pause.*) It's not even something . . .

Dickie   Is it something bad?

Claire   No, it's just . . . I think we need to . . . talk. (*Pause.*) This evening, maybe . . .

Dickie (*pause*)   Yes. (*Pause.*) Yes, I could cook something for us. Get a bottle of plonk. That would be nice. What d'you fancy?

Claire (*pause*)   I'm not hungry.

Dickie   No, but tonight.

Pause. She says nothing.

Well, we'll just play it by ear. Maybe we could splash out. Get a take-away. I could bring back some carbonara. (*Smiles.*) That'd be nice. How about that?

Pause. She nods.

And then we can talk about . . . whatever you want to talk about.

He is putting his new jacket on.

I'll be back about six thirty.

She nods. Pause.

You know, Claire, I . . .

Her eyes shut. Pause. When she opens them again he has gone.

Eleven

*The **Tramp** is reading another letter. **Fliss** hugs him throughout. They remain still in this position. The light in the room changes with the vagaries of the clouds. He finishes it. Pause.*

Tramp   Janis.

Fliss *nods. Pause.*

Tramp   Picture?

Fliss   Picture? (*Pause.*) No, I don't keep pictures. (*Pause.*) But she was very beautiful then.

Tramp   And did I – love her?

Fliss (*pause*)   Oh yes. You did. You loved us both.

Pause. He folds the letter and puts it back into the envelope.

Twelve

A pub. The juke-box plays.

Sid *sits alone, a half-drunk pint in front of him. He is waiting for someone. And then we see who:* **Dickie** *comes in. They stand looking at each other for a moment, nervously. And then, slightly awkwardly,* **Dickie** *leans down to hug his son.* **Sid** *is frozen.*

Lights fade.

Act Two

Thirteen

The pub. **Dickie** *and* **Sid** *sit opposite each other.*
Dickie *raises his glass,* **Sid** *echoes the action half-heartedly.*

Dickie   So. How's things?

Sid *shrugs.*

Dickie   Working?

Sid   Nah. Not really.

Pause. **Dickie** *nods.*

Dickie   But are you liking London?

Sid (*shrugs*)   It's OK.

Dickie *nods. Pause.*

Dickie   But you're getting by?

He nods.

What's your flat like?

Sid   It's a bedsit.

Dickie   A bedsit? (*Pause.*) How much is the rent?

Sid   Too much.

Dickie   But you get it paid?

Sid   Yeah. Pretty much.

Pause. **Dickie** *nods.*

Dickie   Because we hear a lot of bad stories about all
that. We get a lot of lads coming in, complaining that their
giros have been nicked, that they're getting ripped off, all
sorts. Nothing we can do though. It's awful.

Sid   Better than a shop doorway.

Dickie   Oh yes. (*Pause.*) Yes. (*Pause.*) That's the thing: there's more homeless every day it seems. (*Pause.*) Even five years ago you hardly saw any and now ... and all these young kids begging. You're constantly having to turn a blind eye.

Sid   Yeah. That must be awful for you.

A long pause.

Dickie   Still – you're looking well.

Sid   Am I? (*Pause.*) It's amazing what habitual drinking does for you.

Dickie   You don't want to get into that.

Sid   Thou Shalt Not Get Pissed Every Day? ... Hmm. Don't remember that one.

Pause.

Dickie   How's mum?

Sid   Like you give a shit.

Dickie (*pause*)   Do you really believe that? That I don't care?

Sid   There's no evidence to prove you do, is there?

Dickie (*pause*)   What can I say?

Sid   Not a lot.

Dickie   You're not going to tell me how she is?

Sid   Ever heard of a phone?

Dickie   Is that what I should do? Phone her?

Sid (*pause*)   No. (*Pause.*) How is she? (*Pause.*) Well, her husband's left her, she's completely broke and she's so doped up she can barely walk, but apart from that she's just fine. She's actually moving about the house now instead of just staring out the window all day, so I suppose that's what they call an improvement.

A long pause.

No, there's nothing much you can say. I can never think of much myself, when she phones me and tells me how she can't see any future. I've run out of platitudes and philosophies and silver linings and how things can only get ... (*Pause.*) Christ. I don't know why I'm even bothering to tell you this. Doesn't matter to you. You're all right.

Dickie Am I?

Sid You're not alone.

Dickie I go to work. I come home.

Sid To an empty house.

Pause. **Dickie** *nods.*

Oh you do? So what happened to your little girlfriend?

Dickie (*pause*) I've told you before, that was nothing. We were just friends, really.

Sid (*pause*) Christ. You don't change, do you?

Dickie She had nothing to do with my leaving your mother.

Sid Oh come on ...

Dickie The reasons ...

Sid Who are you trying to kid?

Dickie The reasons ...

Sid Is it me you're trying to kid, or is it yourself?

Dickie Sid, the reasons I left your mother are very ... complex, they're twenty-five years' worth of complex ... you can't possibly understand.

Sid Don't tell me I don't understand ... !

Dickie Sid, look ... (*Sighs.*) Your mother – I love her dearly but she moves through life like it's treacle. I know I did some bad things in the beginning but God knows I tried to make up for them! I spent fifteen years trying to make up for them!

Sid   But every time you looked at her all you saw was your own guilt.

Dickie   Well maybe, yes, but do you know how wearing that is? Every man deserves a second chance – we're not born good at living, you have to . . .

Sid   This is all bullshit! Come on, I'm not a little boy any more, why don't you just admit the truth?

Dickie   What's the truth?!

Sid   That you're a sad old man who suddenly, miraculously found himself with a chance of shagging a nice, tight bit of cunt . . . !

Dickie   Don't talk that way.

Sid   Fuck you, I'll talk any fucking, cunting way I like! Nice firm tits, soft skin, no stretch marks, no cellulite – someone who'll listen to your bullshit and tell you that the sun shines out your arse! That's what it comes down to, isn't it?

Dickie *shakes his head.*

Sid   You would've left her anyway, is that what you're saying?

Dickie   Claire was incidental.

Sid   Does she know that?

Dickie   I don't know.

Sid   Because you don't see her?

Dickie (*pause*)   No.

Sid   You're a liar.

Dickie   You don't know anything about it.

Sid   Oh you'd be surprised at what I know.

Pause. **Dickie** *sighs.*

Dickie   Yes. OK. I'm to blame. I probably am.

Sid   The woman that you were supposed to love – and you leave her up there, in a country that you took her to . . .

Dickie   What was I supposed to do? Live a lie?

Sid   Yes! Why not?

Dickie   Then why are you here? If you're so perfect, why didn't you stay with her?

Pause.

Sid   It's not the same. I didn't marry her.

A long pause.

Dickie   All right, Sid. You're not a little boy. But I remember when you were. I remember the first time I saw you in her arms. And I looked at you and I looked at her and I saw my whole life stretch ahead of me and I felt a love – so intense – that it felt like my heart would just – burst. And I thought, yes: a family. Here is my son and here is the woman I will spend the rest of my days with. I felt like I was standing in just exactly my space in the world at just exactly the right time. (*Pause.*) The truth is, I can't tell you how I came to this place from there. What happens in a marriage is a mystery, up there with black holes and God and the *Marie Celeste*. There's nothing can be said, nothing can be done – no judgement we can make on ourselves or on anyone else. You can't change yourself. You can't be considerate. It's pointless. All you can do is make a decision and then take the consequences like a man. And that's what I've done, and that's what I'm doing. For better or for worse.

Sid   Simple as that?

Dickie   Simple doesn't come into it.

Sid *gets up to leave.*

Sid I pity you. I truly do. Because if mum comes through this – when she does, at least she'll have a chance to be happy. But you. You've lost everything. You've lost your wife. You've lost your children. And whatever you have left you'll lose that too.

Dickie (*pause*) Maybe so.

Sid Oh you will. I guarantee it. You'll face up to what you've done, and everything will crumble for you. I promise.

Dickie *stops him from leaving. He embraces* **Sid** *who cannot respond.*

Dickie Please don't hate me, Sid. I love your mother. I love you too. Please believe me. However it seems.

He disengages. He brushes **Sid**'s *hair with his hand.*

Sid I know she wants to kill herself. I know she does. And you know the worst thing? The worst most terrible thing? Sometimes I wish she would.

Sid *leaves him there alone.*

Fourteen

The screeching of brakes again and the terrible impact. The **Tramp** *is huddled in a corner, his hands over his face. He is shaking violently. He gets up, paces frantically backwards and forwards. He tries the doors he tries the windows, all locked. The sound of the car again and again. He is raging. He huddles in the corner again. Eventually,* **Fliss** *enters, rushing to him.*

Fliss Oh, Daddy!

She holds him as he shakes, she makes comforting noises.

It's all right, Fliss is here now. Ssshh. It's all right. Was it the crash again?

He nods, gripping her.

It's all right. You're safe.

Tramp Drink!

Fliss Now, now. You don't need that.

Tramp (*nods*) Please!

Fliss I know it's hard, but you'll be better soon. You have to be strong.

The car screeching. The impact. He buries his face in her, terrified.

Tramp Stop it!

Fliss What do you see? Is it the crash?

He shakes his head he doesn't know.

The other car? The burning man?

Tramp I don't know! Stop it!

He pulls away from her and goes to the locked window. He tries the locked door.

Fliss It's for your own good. Trust me. I know you want to get away. It's the truth you're afraid of. You've been hiding for years. You have to be strong.

He bangs at the door. She goes to him, restraining him.

Daddy!

He turns on her.

Tramp No!

Fliss Yes!

Tramp I'm not!

Fliss You are!

He shakes his head.

Then who are you?

Tramp I don't know!

Fliss You're Henry Gaines . . .

Tramp   No!

Fliss   Yes. I know you're in pain but it'll stop once you know who you are, I promise. You want it to stop, don't you?

He holds her. His legs giving way. He sobs.

You're Henry Gaines. Just keep saying it to yourself. You know who you are, you're Henry Gaines. Say it.

He shakes his head, his face buried in her skirt.

I know it's hard but I'm here now. I won't let anything happen to you. Just say it 'I'm Henry Gaines'.

Again he shakes his head. She strokes his hair. Pause. Then she pulls gently away from him. She goes to her bag, him grovelling after her. She produces a letter. As he sees it he calms.

(*Nods.*) It's the next letter.

Pause. He stops his groaning.

Would you like to read it? The next letter from Janis?

Pause. He nods, crawling towards her. She holds it away from him.

Say it then. Say it and you can read the next letter.

A long pause.

Say 'I know who I am.'

Tramp   I know . . . who I am.

Fliss   I'm Henry Gaines.

Tramp   (*pause*)   I'm . . . Henry Gaines.

Fliss   (*pause*)   Who are you?

Tramp   I'm Henry Gaines.

Pause. She offers him the letter. He takes it as a starving man receives bread.

I'm Henry Gaines.

He holds the letter against his cheek.

Henry Gaines.

Fifteen

Claire *and* **Dickie**'s *flat.*

Claire *and* **Sid** *enter.*

Claire   I don't know about this, Sid. This isn't right.

Sid   So this is where you disappear to. Your little love nest.

He wanders around, smiling.

Very nice. (*Pause.*) Girls' things. Flowery things. Patterned things. Living things. I almost feel sorry for him. (*Pause.*) Nothing lonelier than a room that once had girls' things in it.

Claire   All right, Sid. You've seen it. Can we go now?

Sid   Relax.

Claire   Relax?

Sid   He won't be back for ages.

Claire   He might be.

Sid   What difference does it make? You're going to chuck him.

A long pause.

Claire   It's still not right.

Sid   Lots of things aren't 'right'. Leaving your wife for a girl half her age isn't 'right'. Doesn't sound like a man who's concerned with what's 'right', old Dickie.

Claire (*pause*)   His name is Richard.

Sid   Maybe you're getting cold feet. Maybe it's him you want to be with, not me.

She doesn't answer.

Pardon?

Claire   No.

Sid   He's no friend of mine. Caused me a lot of pain.

Claire   What pain's he caused you?

Sid (*pause*)   More than you know.

Claire   It's me that's caused you pain. (*Pause.*) He's not a bad man.

Sid   What the fuck do you know?

Claire   I know him.

Sid   Nobody knows anyone.

He walks up behind her. Starts to kiss her neck.

Claire   Sid – please – let's go.

Sid   What's wrong?

Claire   Not here.

Sid   You know something.

Claire   What?

Sid   I don't believe you. I don't believe you're going to finish with him.

She nods. Her eyes closed as he kisses her.

Sid   I think you're going to string us both along. Is that right?

He bites her tongue and she yelps.

Claire   No. I'm going to.

Sid   Because I'm getting a bit –

He bites her again.

– sick of all this. You've had your way for too long. So I'm giving you an ultimatum: You finish with him . . .

Claire   Please – Sid –

Sid Tonight. You finish with him tonight or it's all over between us, you understand?

He bites down on her shoulder.

You understand?

She nods.

Over. As in never see me, never talk to me, never hear of me again. Is that what you want?

Claire You know it isn't.

Sid Then you end it tonight. You understand?

Claire (*nods*) Now can we please go?

Sid What do you care? He doesn't mean anything to you. That's what you said.

Claire I'm going to finish with him. Isn't that enough?

Sid No. I want you to prove yourself.

Claire This is bad, Sid.

Sid You're a bad girl.

He smacks her behind. She closes her eyes, smiling despite herself.

Claire Don't.

Sid Admit it. You're a bad girl.

He smacks her again harder. She exclaims. She turns and kisses him.

Claire I am a bad girl.

He undoes his belt. She watches him.

Claire What are you doing?

Sid Bad girls deserve to have their cunts licked for an hour at least.

She shudders with the crudity of his words. He removes his belt, kissing her.

Are you a bad girl?

Claire   What if he comes back?

Sid   Are you a bad girl?

He loops the belt around her neck. She nods.

How bad?

Claire (*smiles*)   Very bad.

Sid   How bad?

Claire   An hour's worth of bad.

Sid   A piece of shit?

Claire (*nods*)   A total piece of shit.

Sid   Where do you fuck? In the bedroom? (*Pause.*) Where is it?

Involuntarily her eyes wander to the bedroom. Smiling he leads her by the belt towads it. They exit the room. Light changes. Music plays. And . . .

After a time **Dickie** *comes in, just to drop off his briefcase before he goes out to get food. It's as well that he's wearing a walkman or he'd hear the sound of his son and his girlfriend. He leaves again.*

Sixteen

Fliss *is reading to the* **Tramp** *from a history book. Gradually he starts to slouch in his seat. he seems bored. Eventually* **Fliss** *stops reading.*

Fliss   You're slouching again.

Pause. He corrects himself. She walks over to him, adjusts him.

Like this. That's it. (*Pause.*) Posture was very important to you. You couldn't stand people slouching.

She sits down again, starts to read. Slowly, we see him begin to slouch. She stares at him. He straightens. Without noticing he begins to bite one of his nails. She slams the book shut.

No no no!

He looks at her innocently.

Get your fingers out of your mouth! (*Pause.*) Take your
fingers out of your mouth!

She walks over to him, inspects his hands. Angry, she smacks them.

Look at your nails, they're horrible! You never bit your
nails! You never slouched and you never bit your nails!

He pulls his hands away, angry. Pause. She sighs.

I'm sorry. I know this is difficult. You've picked up a lot of
bad habits. I understand that. But if you want to be like
you were then you have to remember what I tell you. It'll
be hard at first, but eventually it'll be like second nature.

Pause. He looks sulky.

If you have to do something with your hands, then rub
your chin. You used to do that. Try that.

Pause. He rubs his chin.

No, more like:

She rubs her chin slowly.

In a more thoughtful way, you were a teacher remember?
All your movements were deep and graceful and mature.
You would never bite your nails or pick your nose or
anything like that, never. Try it again.

*Pause. He rubs his chin slowly, thoughtfully. He does it a few times,
he gets it right.*

Yes! That's more like it! Now doesn't that feel more
natural?

He nods, unconvinced.

Tramp   Can I see the next letter?

Fliss (*pause*)   A little more reading first.

He shifts petulantly in his seat.

What's wrong?

Tramp   I don't understand it.

Fliss   What do you mean you don't understand it? You used to teach it.

A long pause.

Tramp   I need a drink.

Fliss   What, some tea?

Tramp (*pause*)   A drink.

Fliss (*pause*)   Now you know that's not allowed. You can't have another letter because you simply don't deserve it. You can have a card.

She picks out a card and tosses it to him, contemptuously. She leaves the room.

He looks at the card but it takes only a moment to read. He stares at it disappointed.

From the other room, **Fliss** *yelps with pain. She comes in limping rubbing her knee.*

Fliss   Oh – I hurt myself! I hurt myself!

She hobbles over to him.

I was making you some tea and banged my knee right on the sore bit!

He doesn't respond. She is pouting like a child.

Look – it's all red.

She lifts her skirt and shows him her knee, bringing it up to his face. He pats it. This is not enough.

Kiss it, Daddy. Kiss it better.

Pause. He kisses it. She smiles, and sits on his knee. She takes the card from him and lets it fall on the floor. Pause.

I'm sorry for shouting at you. (*Pause.*) Do you forgive me?

Pause. He nods. She hugs him, nestling her head against him.

You are happy here, aren't you?

Pause. He nods.

I'm happy too.

Tramp   I loved her? Janis.

Pause. She nods.

Fliss   Tomorrow we can go for a walk. There's a park where you used to take me . . .

Tramp   She was my wife?

Fliss   Yes. You know she was. But this park, it's beautiful – it's got all these sculpted . . .

Tramp   Where is she?

Fliss   All these sculpted hedgerows in the shape of . . .

Tramp   Felicity.

Pause. She looks at him.

Where is she? (*Pause.*) Can I see her?

Pause.

Fliss (*nods*)   In time.

Tramp   Now.

Fliss (*shakes head*)   Not now.

Tramp   Why not?

Fliss   Because you're not . . . ready yet.

Tramp   I loved her. She loved me.

Fliss   In time.

Tramp   Now.

Fliss   Please, Daddy. Just trust me.

Tramp   Janis.

Fliss *stands angrily.*

Fliss   Will you stop going on!

Tramp   She loved me.

Fliss   I'm the one who found you! She didn't believe me! Nobody did! So she can just wait.

Tramp (*pause*)   Please.

Fliss (*sighs*)   Look – Daddy – I didn't want to tell you this but I can see you're going to push me until I do:

A long pause.

Mum died three years ago, of breast cancer.

A long pause.

I'm sorry. I didn't want to tell you yet. (*Pause.*) It's just us.

Pause. He points at the bag with the letters inside. She follows his finger.

(*Pause.*) I don't think you should read another. Not right now. (*Pause.*) Oh stupid Fliss, I shouldn't have shown you them at all, should I? I just thought . . .

He does not retract his hand.

(*Tearful.*) Please, Daddy. Don't. You've still got me. I'm enough for you, aren't I? She'd be so happy that we're together now. It'd be like a dream come true. She wouldn't want you to be sad. All she'd want is for us to get better, to remember. All she'd want is for you to take care of me.

Still he just stares at the letters, his hand outstretched.

Daddy, my knee's sore. It's got sore again. I think I've done something to it.

Again she puts her knee up in front of him. He kisses it in a perfunctory manner, reaching for the letters.

It's not just my knee now. It's spread.

She raises her skirt further. Her thigh. Only now does the **Tramp**'s *hand lower. He looks at her.*

It's there too.

She pouts. A long pause. She takes his hand and gently places it on her thigh.

Just there. Was that bad cupboard door hurt Fliss.

She pauses like that, with his hand on her thigh. Then sits on his knee again, hugging him.

Bounce me. Bounce me, Daddy.

And he does.

Seventeen

At the bus stop. **Claire** *and* **Dickie**. *It's raining. He steps out to look down the street.*

Dickie   Another 41. Can you believe that?

A long pause.

How are you feeling now?

She nods.

Stomach still sore?

Claire (*pause*)   A bit.

Dickie   Food wasn't so good anyway. I'm sure that was tinned ham. (*Pause.*) That's the thing about pasta – it was always what we ate when we were skint. Seems funny to pay through the nose for it. (*Pause.*) Pasta and corned beef hash. And Lara used to make this fish pie – God it was awful. Me and my son used to scrape it out the window when she wasn't looking. But we used to laugh so much, it always gave the game away.

Long pause.

Maybe we should just get a cab. It won't be that much.

Claire (*pause*)   I'm not coming back.

Dickie   Hmmm?

Claire   I'm not coming back.

Dickie (*pause*)   What do you mean?

Claire   Dickie – listen – (*Pause.*) I've been seeing someone else.

A long pause. He smiles grimly, unconvincingly. He steadies himself. Slowly he exhales air.

Dickie   Going down. Basement for haberdashery, perfume et cetera.

A long pause.

How long?

Claire   Three months or so.

Pause.

Dickie   I didn't need to know this.

Claire   I can't go on lying.

Dickie   Why not?

Claire   It's not fair on you.

Dickie   That's your problem.

Claire   You knew.

Dickie   You slept with him?

Claire   What's the point in this?

Dickie   You started it, now I have to know the details. I have to know if we have anything special left.

Claire   I haven't slept with him.

A long pause.

Dickie   Oh God, Claire. Oh God.

Music builds louder and louder. The actors continue to improvise the breaking-up scene, but mute now, playing out the actions.

Eventually **Claire** *leaves* **Dickie** *standing there alone, and the music ends.*

Eighteen

Claire *is at* **Sid**'s.

Sid   So how did he take it?

Claire (*pause*)   He took it all right.

Pause.

Sid   Did he cry?

Claire (*pause*)   Did he cry?

Sid (*nods*)   And did he sob when he did? Or was he quiet? Did he swallow it down?

Pause.

Claire   Why are you asking me this?

Sid (*pause*)   Did he say romantic things? Or was he angry? Did he beg with you to stay?

Pause.

See, it's a funny thing: I went into a church today, fuck knows why. But inside it was empty, all stone and full of dust but the sun was . . . streaming in through the stained glass windows so there were these . . . colours just shimmering in the air now and then, when the dust swirled – red and green – like a wee rainbow indoors. I had my camera but it was too delicate to catch. And I really wanted to say to someone – 'look at that.' (*Pause.*) It wasn't enough for me to see it for myself. Like it wouldn't be real enough unless someone else saw it. (*Pause.*) And that's the thing about losing people, you lose the things that make you real. You lose half those moments. You lose your past. You don't move and you don't speak because you've lost your past.

A long pause.

So have you moved out?

Claire (*pause*) I suppose I have.

Sid So where are you going to stay?

Claire (*pause*) Don't know. Debbie's I suppose.

Sid Have you phoned her?

Claire (*pause*) Maybe tomorrow.

Sid So where are you going to stay tonight?

Claire (*pause*) Tonight?

Sid (*nods*) That's the dark bit between now and tomorrow.

A long pause.

Claire Well can't I stay here?

Sid (*smiles*) No – you see – I stay here.

Claire (*pause*) Are you serious?

A long pause.

Sid?

Sid (*pause*) What d'you think this is, Claire? Musical chairs? I – I – I – I – I'm not your stepping stone – You get me?

Claire (*amazed*) I'm just talking about tonight.

Sid No you're not just talking about tonight, you're talking about tonight and tomorrow night and every night until you forget for a moment that it's pain you want, that it's pain you need and you hop to the next man and then you remember that happiness is beyond you, that happiness and love are beyond the likes of you and me. (*Pause.*) I mean, what's your story, Claire? What's your family tree? What's your fuck-up?

Claire   Sid . . . Why are you . . .

Sid   I mean, you talk about how fucked up your sister is.
I mean, is there a history of madness in your family? Or
was it some primal moment? A sweetie refused? A wasp in
your cot, a harsh word when you wet the bed? Or was it
warring parents, cutting chunks out of each other whilst
you try to watch the telly? Did you think it was like that in
every house? Come on, Claire! What's your fuck-up? Let's
get to the bottom of this! School, maybe – where you
learned to keep secrets, where you learn the thrill of lying
wanking off some teenager's cock in your flowery bedroom,
letting him poke his fingers up you whilst your parents sit
downstairs, just the sheer thrill of everything that's bad and
wicked and foul. Are we getting warmer? Or are we tip-
toeing into the land of the seriously dysfunctional? Is there
summat nasty int' woodshed? And are we talking genetic
deformity, inherited disease or could it be . . . ? The Holy
Grail? The Iron Cross? Not . . . child abuse?

Pause.

Yes, old Brian, old counsellor Brian – I can see him now
in his cloak and horns, standing on his pentangle – and
there's wee Claire on the altar in her birthday suit. Is that
it? Or was it worse that that? Was it Fliss on the altar,
whilst Claire peeled the potatoes, was that it? Daddy
spending all his time with another man's daughter,
spending all the time he should be spending on you? Not
that I blame him. She's a looker your sister. I could fill a
chalice for her myself. Or hey! maybe I'm in luck. Maybe
we've got a bit of sisterly incest going on, in which case
you can count me in. I'd happily be the marge in a Fliss
and Claire sandwich. You ever think about that? The two
of you taking turns on me. I'll watch, you share a banana.
Me on the wrist expanders. And then you watch me and
her whilst we . . .

*She slaps him. Stunned pause. She slaps him again, many times. He
remains impassive. She starts to cry. (The actress should improvise her
response.)*

*Slowly **Sid** picks up his camera and starts taking photos of her in her distress.*

This shuts her up. She stares at him, disbelieving – backs away from him and leaves.

***Sid** is still taking photos after she's gone, recording the empty space where she once stood.*

Nineteen

*The **Tramp** stands at the window, looking out.*

Fliss   Try again. You almost had it.

Tramp   I don't feel like it.

Fliss   But that's the point: if you do it then you'll feel more like doing it again.

Tramp   Why won't you tell me where she's buried?

Fliss (*sighs*)   Why do you have to go on?! (*Pause.*) The sooner we get this done the sooner you can read some more letters. In fact, I had a special treat for you today – a postcard you sent from John O'Groats.

Pause. He looks at her. She nods, smiling.

So why don't we try again?

A long pause and then he laughs at nothing. Pause, she nods.

Yes, but deeper, more:

She tries to imitate the laugh. He tries it a couple of times without putting much effort into it.

You're not really trying.

Tramp   I don't feel like laughing.

She sulks, puffing. A long pause.

Fliss   All right. (*Pause.*) We could play Twister again.

Tramp   Not again!

Fliss   It was fun, wasn't it?

Tramp   Yes but my back's sore.

Fliss   It's important! It's important that we play together. A postcard must be worth a game of Twister at least!

Pause.

Operation then.

Tramp   How do you know these things about me?

Fliss   Which things?

Tramp   How I laugh, how I rub my chin. You don't remember them, do you?

Fliss   Maybe I do, I don't know whether I do or whether I just remember Janis telling me. But they're true, I do know that.

Tramp (*pause*)   Why don't you let me visit her? I have to visit her.

Fliss   Why do you have to visit her?!

Tramp   Because I loved her. She loved me!

Fliss   But you don't love her any more. Do you?

He says nothing.

You can't possibly! You don't even remember her!

Tramp (*pause*)   I remember . . . something.

Fliss (*pause*)   What?

Tramp   A feeling.

Fliss   How do you know it was a feeling about her?

Pause. He doesn't.

Tramp   I still have to see her. (*Pause.*) Please.

Fliss   If you want anything from me, you'd better start being more co-operative! I know she's important to you but

it's Janis this – Janis that. (*Pause.*) I don't want you to be
let down. She wasn't any angel, you know. It's not as if she
just sat at home and pined for you after you died.
Disappeared. (*Pause.*) You might as well know ... she
married someone else.

Pause. The **Tramp** *stares at her.*

Her counsellor, can you believe that? Within two years she
was married to him and having another baby. So she can't
have loved you that much can she?

Tramp (*pause*)   Did she love him?

Fliss   I suppose she must have. But I always knew he
wasn't my daddy. I never sat on his knee or anything. He
liked me to but I wouldn't.

Tramp (*pause*)   What was he like?

Fliss   Horrible. (*Shudders.*) He was horrible. (*Pause.*) I didn't
tell you so we could talk about him, I just want you to
know the truth.

A long pause.

Tramp   It doesn't matter. I still want to visit her grave.

Fliss   Well, you can't, unless I take you!

Tramp   Then take me.

Fliss (*shakes head*)   Not yet.

Tramp   I'm your father and I'm telling you to take me.

Fliss   I've told you – it's just us now!

Tramp   Take me there, Felicity.

Fliss   But she's not interested in you! She doesn't care!
She doesn't believe me!

Pause.

Didn't believe me. When she was alive. Which she isn't
now. (*Pause.*) She's dead three years ago. Of lung cancer.

Tramp (*pause*)   Breast cancer.

Fliss (*nods*)   Lung and breast cancer. Both of them. It was awful.

Pause.

You are impossible! You've got me all muddled up! Well, it's about time you remembered why you're here and who brought you here, in off the streets into this nice place. If it wasn't for me you'd be nothing, you'd have nothing. You'd just be a piece of shit lying in shit. Well, you can forget about reading any more letters!

She starts putting her coat on.

I'm going out. You can just sit here and stew until I get back. And you'd better do some thinking whilst I'm gone!

Tramp   Don't lock me in!

But she does. He sits down, glumly. Eventually he starts talking to himself.

Hello, pleased to meet you. I'm Henry Gaines. Hello. And this is my wife Janis Gaines. Pardon? Oh thank you, yes, she is very beautiful, yes. She's a student you know. Oh yes, very brainy. And I'm a teacher too. I teach History. Yes she is. Very lovely. Her hair is black and her face is round and she says some very nice things about me I can tell you. Sends me letters and cards. Yes, my dear wife. And we have a daughter, don't we, dear? Felicity. By the way, have you heard the new Dylan album? It's quite different. I like it.

The illusion falls away.

Twenty

*As the **Tramp** stands there, we bring the lights up, first on **Dickie**, and then on **Sid**. Three lost men, each in their own space.*

Sid *finishes off a bottle of gin and reels unsteadily out of the door.*

Twenty-One

The **Tramp** *is desperately trying to open the small chest that contains the letters, but without luck. Then he hears the door unlock.* **Claire** *enters.*

A long pause as they stare at each other warily. Simultaneous:

Tramp
Claire } Who are you?

Pause.

Tramp ⎫ I'm Henry, Fliss's –
Claire ⎭ I'm Claire, Fliss's –

Pause.

Claire   Sister. (*Pause.*) Where's Fliss?

Tramp   She locked me in.

Claire   Who are you?

Tramp   You're her sister?

She nods.

I'm Henry Gaines. I'm her father. (*Pause.*) You're not my daughter too, are you?

Claire   No. I'm not.

Tramp   Can you help me?

Pause.

I have to know where she's buried.

Claire   Where who's buried?

Tramp   Janis.

Claire   Janis? (*Pause.*) Mum? (*Pause.*) She lives in France.

Tramp (*shakes head*)   No. She's dead.

Claire   She lives in France. I should know. (*Pause.*) Did Fliss say she was dead?

Pause. He nods.

Who are you really?

Tramp (*pause*)   Can you take me to her?

Claire   To Janis? (*Pause.*)   Why?

Tramp   She was ... my wife.

Pause.

Claire   Where did she find you?

Pause. He looks out the window.

Christ, Fliss. You mad cow. (*Pause.*) What's she done?
Drugged you? (*Pause.*) She told you you're her father?

Tramp (*pause*)   I'm Henry Gaines.

Claire   Fliss's dad died when she was two. She never
even knew him ...

Tramp   She showed me letters. They said nice things
about me.

Claire   Look. I'm sorry. I don't know if you're just
bluffing, but you should know that my sister's not ... right.
She's never been right. I don't know what she's told you
but Henry Gaines died when she was two ...

Tramp (*nods*)   In a crash. I remember a crash.

Claire   There's a thousand crashes every day. (*Pause.*)
She's kept you locked in here? (*Pause.*) Christ. (*Pause.*) Don't
you remember anything else?

Tramp   She loved me. Janis. I remember loving her.

Claire   You remember her face?

Tramp (*pause*)   Dark hair, round face ...

Claire (*shakes head*)   Blonde hair. Like mine.

The **Tramp** *repeats some Greek history.*

Claire   Look, I understand – a pretty girl, a nice place to stay, plenty of food. But it's not right to feed these mad ideas she has.

He just stares at her.

You believe it, don't you? (*Pause.*) What about the crash? You say you remember a crash? Can you remember what happened?

He starts to pace uncomfortably.

Tramp   I'm Henry Gaines.

Claire   What do you remember about this crash?

Faintly, the sound of screeching brakes. The **Tramp** *brushes at his ear as if to ward off a wasp.*

Tramp   Crash ...

Claire   If you can remember it maybe we can ...

His hands go to his ears. The brakes get louder and louder. He is frightened.

Tramp   Oh no – no!

He cowers.

Claire   What's wrong?

The brakes scream now until the impact, louder than ever before. **Claire** *hesitantly approaches him, trying to calm him. Straight after the sound of the impact, he babbles.*

Tramp   I'm drunk!

Claire   Are you?

Tramp   I'm drunk – I'm driving – the lights are red – all blurred – red and green – ... in the air – getting faster – straight ahead – no road – it's black – a wall – my foot's down – the wheel – the wall gets – bigger – bigger ...

His body jolts with the imaginary impact.

CLAIRE! CLAIRE!

He hugs her tight, she struggles. And then **Fliss** *enters. Sees this.*

Fliss   GET AWAY FROM HIM!

She rushes over, pulling **Claire** *away from him.*

What have you done to him? What has she done to you?

Claire   What have I done to him?

Fliss   This isn't your business, Claire! I asked you for help and you wouldn't, so what are you doing here?

Claire   I needed somewhere to stay.

Fliss   Well, you can't stay here! You can just give me back my keys! You wouldn't help me so I don't see why I should help you!

Claire   Fliss – you can't just kidnap people and fuck up their heads!

Fliss   What have you been saying to him? Daddy, whatever she said it's not true!

Claire   You told him mum was dead.

Fliss (*gasps*)   Oh you! She is dead.

Claire   She's not – don't say that!

Fliss   Well, I had to say it, Daddy! I had to! She wouldn't help me and I want you to see her but she won't listen to me and she's not here and it was Claire who made her go anyway!

Claire   That's not true! If she hadn't been such a little tramp there'd have been nothing to tell!

Fliss   Don't listen to her, she just wants to spoil this for me! She doesn't want me to have anything!

Claire   What do you mean?! What did I have? Nothing! You took everything from me! Everything I ever have she takes away from me!

Fliss   You see, Daddy?! That's why she's saying all this.

Claire   Don't you see what a fake she is? That fake face, that fake voice . . . !

Fliss It's her voice that's fake, not mine! (*Pause.*) Wanted to sound more 'working class'!

Claire She's always had everything – money, success, skinny little legs!

Fliss You were the pretty one! Always good at school, always got nice boyfriends. I didn't have anything – I didn't even have a daddy and now I find you and so she wants to take you away!

Claire Like you did to me?!

Fliss It wasn't my fault he was horrible!

Claire He wasn't, you loved every minute of it!

Fliss I did not! I didn't, Daddy! The only reason Brian left was because she told!

Claire I had to!

Fliss She just did it to get me into trouble! But then it backfired because he went away, and then Janis went away, they all went away and it was her fault!

Claire Wasn't!

Fliss Was! And even so, I was always nice to you. I gave you money. I sent you a Valentine's card every year. And now I prove you all wrong and you're so jealous . . .

Claire Jealous?! Why would I be jealous? He's not even your . . .

Fliss *hums very loudly obscuring this. Pause.*

Claire He's not even your . . .

Fliss *covers* **Claire**'s *mouth, desperately. They start to tussle. It's ridiculous. Eventually, the* **Tramp** *stands.*

Tramp Felicity! Claire! Both of you! . . . Stop it!

Pause. They stop.

Let go of each other.

They do. They look ashamed. Pause.

Fliss   But she was the one that . . .

Tramp   Be QUIET! (*Pause.*) This isn't fair! I'm a person! Whoever I am, wherever I came from, I'm a person! I'm brainy now and I've got letters and I sit up straight just like any other person! I watch *EastEnders*! I'm a person!

Pause.

Fliss   You wouldn't watch *EastEnders*.

Tramp   Well I do watch *EastEnders*! I LIKE *Eastenders*!

Pause. The phone rings. They all listen.

Claire   What's that?

Fliss   The phone.

Pause. **Fliss** *looks at her watch.*

Claire   Who would phone at this time?

Pause. **Fliss** *shakes her head.*

Are you going to answer it?

Fliss   It's probably nothing. Probably a wrong number.

Pause. She goes to answer it leaving **Claire** *with the* **Tramp**.

Tramp   I have to meet Janis. It feels like I'll die if I don't. Can you help me?

Pause. **Fliss** *comes back in looking puzzled.*

Claire   What is it?

Fliss   Claire, it's the police.

Claire   The police?

Fliss (*nods*)   Don't panic – but there's been a accident.

Claire (*pause*)   Who?

Fliss   Someone called . . . James something . . .

Claire (*pause*)   I don't know anyone called James.

Fliss   Well, he told them to contact you. They want you to go down to hospital.

Claire   But I don't know any James.

Fliss   Go and talk to them.

Pause. Bewildered, she does so leaving **Fliss** *with the* **Tramp**.

Fliss   Oh how terrible. These roads. So many people dying on these roads.

Twenty-Two

Claire *waits in hospital.* **Dickie** *enters. He rushes. He rushes up to her and hugs her.*

Claire   Dickie . . . !?

Dickie   Oh God, Claire – it's terrible – Got to find out what ward he's in. Do you know what ward he's in?

Claire (*pause*)   Look I can cope with this on my own.

Dickie   Don't be stupid, Claire. What ward's he in?

Claire (*pause*)   Ward five.

Dickie   Where is it?

Claire   Well, it's upstairs . . .

Dickie   Right . . .

She grabs him.

Claire   Dickie, don't you dare – What's the point in this, he's fucked.

Dickie   He's fucked?!

Pause.

Claire   How did you find me here?

Dickie (*pause*)   What are you talking about?

Long pause.

Twenty-Three

Fliss *is depressed. She unlocks the small chest and carries the letters over to the* **Tramp**.

Fliss   That's them all. Read them when you like.

She starts to leave.

Tramp   Where are you going?

Fliss (*pause*)   I'm going to bed.

Pause. She continues on. He stops her.

Please, I tried my best. I can't get her to come. I know you'll want to go and find her. (*Pause.*) All I wanted was . . .

She drifts off into a glaze. He tugs her back. Pause.

See I get these funny moods. They're hard to explain. (*Pause.*) It's like I'm a tiny pin-prick of light in a huge black . . . sea. (*Pause.*) So I'm as well going to bed. You probably don't trust anything I say now anyway. (*Pause.*) I haven't locked the door.

Tramp   Felicity?

Pause.

What colour are my eyes?

She bends down to look.

Fliss   Brown. (*Pause.*) Why?

A long pause. She looks a bit nervous.

Why?

Pause.

Tramp   I'd forgotten. (*Pause.*) Tomorrow we could go for that walk. What do you think?

Pause. She nods, smiling faintly. She exits, leaving the **Tramp** *there with the letters.*

Twenty-Four

Sid *sits in a chair, obviously brain-damaged.* **Dickie** *is feeding him.*

Dickie   There's a boy. A little more? Come on –

He wipes at **Sid***'s chin, puts the food down.*

Never mind, you've done well.

Pause.

They've put all the Christmas lights on in town. It's quite spectacular. Maybe we'll go down and look at them sometime. You used to love the Christmas lights. You got so excited. Late-night shopping, you in your little hat, the lights on your face and if it was snowing – ! That was the best of all.

Dickie *takes the plate to the kitchen.*

Claire *comes in. She stands there, not knowing where to look.*
Dickie *comes back and sees her. Pause. He goes to* **Sid***, strokes his hair.*

Dickie   Look who's come to see us, Jimmy.

Claire   Look, I can't stay – there's a car waiting.

Dickie   Your stuff is all ready to go, I think that's everything.

Claire   Yeah, thanks. I'm sorry it took so long.

Dickie   Who's waiting, Fliss?

Claire   No, I'm staying at Debbie's.

Dickie (*pause*)   Debbie. (*Pause.*) You OK?

Claire   Yes. (*Pause.*) So have you had to give up work for . . .

Dickie   He's a full-time job. It's all right though. (*Pause.*) It's nice to see you, Claire. Isn't it nice to see Claire? I've got something for you: a present.

Claire   I don't want it.

Dickie   It'll only take a minute.

Claire   No, I've really got to go.

Dickie   It says for Claire. That must be you.

Claire *takes the tape.* **Dickie** *gives her a Walkman.* **Claire** *listens to half the tape, stops it.*

Dickie   Do you like it?

Claire   Yeah I do, thank you.

Dickie   Don't thank me. It was in his pocket the night of the accident. I listened to it.

Claire *listens to the rest of the song. Originally, 'The Most Beautiful Girl in the World' by Charlie Rich was used. But whatever is used, the lyrics should convey* **Sid***'s love for* **Claire***.*

Claire *takes the headphones off. Pause.*

Dickie   So what are you doing for Christmas?

Claire   Fliss wants me to spend it with her, but I don't know.

Dickie   Then you should. (*Pause.*) What, do you mind spending it with her?

Claire   No, not really.

Dickie   Then if you don't mind and it makes her happy, spend Christmas with her, she's your sister. (*Pause.*) If you weren't going to Fliss's, I was going to suggest you might like to come here, I know Jimmy would like that.

Claire   No, you're right, I should spend it with Fliss.

Dickie   No chance he could come to you then, just for a couple of hours. (*Pause.*) I won't come, if that's what you're worried about. I just think it would be good for him. I think he cared about you, despite what it seems. (*Pause.*) This is ridiculous, I've no right to ask, it's totally out of order, sorry, I'll get your stuff.

Dickie *exits.* **Claire** *goes to* **Sid**, *slaps him. She sits down again.* **Dickie** *comes back in, gives her some bags. Pause.*

Claire　If I was to ask Fliss and she was to say it was all right, would you do something for me?

Dickie　Anything.

Claire　Anything?

Long pause.

Twenty-Five

Christmas Day. A table is set. The **Tramp** *is carefully doing up his tie.* **Fliss** *enters. She too is dressed up and carrying five glasses. She puts them on the table. Behind them a Christmas tree sits there, its coloured lights glowing.*

Tramp　How's this?

Fliss *inspects his tie. She smiles.*

Fliss　Perfect. I knew it would suit you. (*Pause.*) You look lovely.

Tramp　No, it's you that looks lovely.

She smiles. Pause, as they gaze at each other.

How's the turkey?

Fliss　It's definitely dead now.

Tramp　I'm sorry, Fliss. It looked dead when he gave it to me.

Fliss　You weren't to know. But you shouldn't buy turkeys from strangers.

Tramp He said it was free-range.

Fliss Even so.

Tramp When's Claire coming?

Fliss She should be here any minute. She ordered a taxi when she phoned. So you'll have to help her in with her friend. I hope they get here before the Queen's speech.

She stares at him fondly. Long pause.

Tramp What's wrong?

Fliss Nothing. Nothing's wrong.

Tramp You're acting a bit strangely.

Fliss Am I. (*Pause.*) Well, it's Christmas Day.

Pause. He nods.

Tramp Don't you like your present?

Fliss I do. I love it. It's just a bit hot in the kitchen for a Shetland jumper.

Tramp It gets cold at night though. You've got to wrap up warm.

Fliss It'll be just the thing.

Pause. Again she stares at him.

Tramp Are you sure there's nothing wrong?

Fliss (*pause*) I'm sure. There's nothing wrong. There's nothing wrong anywhere in the world.

Pause. She runs to the window, looks out.

That's her.

*She exits. The **Tramp** looks suspiciously at the five glasses on the table.*

Fliss (*offstage*) Daddy? Come and help.

Pause. He exits.

Twenty-Six

Sid/James *now sits at the table, unmoving. The* **Tramp** *is out of breath still. A small 'snowstorm' ornament sits in* **Sid***'s lap.* **Claire** *shakes it for him.* **Fliss** *is opening her present, it's a hat.*

Fliss   Oh, Claire! How lovely!

She puts it on and turns to the **Tramp***.*

Fliss   What do you think?

Tramp   It's very nice.

Fliss   It's lovely. Thank you.

She goes to her sister, hugs her.

Thank you, Claire.

A long pause.

You didn't have to give me anything else though. You couldn't give me a better present than this. (*Pause.*) You know I love you, don't you? Whatever happens I always will.

Pause. **Claire** *nods.* **Fliss** *kisses her hand.*

Did you like your presents? I know it's not much but . . .

Claire (*nods*)   Knickers always come in handy.

Fliss   But you don't like the book, do you?

Claire   It's fine, it's just – I don't have cellulite.

Fliss   No, but that's how it goes: one minute you haven't, the next . . . but the exercises are good for your thighs anyway.

Pause. **Claire** *nods. She turns to* **Sid***.*

Claire   Say thank you for your snowstorm, Sid.

He doesn't respond.

He says thank you.

Fliss From the way you were talking about him I thought he was . . . younger.

Claire He did a painting for you.

She produces the painting. A few zigzag lines on paper. She gives it to **Fliss***.*

Fliss That's very . . . nice. (*To* **Sid**.) That's very nice. (*Pause.*) How did he do it?

Claire It's a mouth painting.

Fliss (*to* **Sid**) Whose mouth is it?

Claire No, he painted it with his mouth. Holding the brush in his mouth.

Fliss So he can move his head then?

Claire (*pause*) No. (*Pause.*) I had to give him some help.

Claire *makes a gentle slapping gesture. Pause.* **Fliss** *puts the painting down.*

Fliss Anyway, I think it's about time to eat, don't you?

She ushers the **Tramp** *into his seat.*

All right, potatoes should be ready now. Shall I be mother?

Claire Want a hand.

Fliss No, no, don't you dare. (*Pause.*) Maybe you could pour some drinks.

Fliss *exits.* **Claire** *and the* **Tramp** *exchange glances.*

Twenty-Seven

After dinner. They all have drinks. A straw in **Sid***'s mouth. He's had his own food. A devastated carcase sits before them. The* **Tramp** *dabs his mouth with a hanky.*

They are playing charades. **Fliss** *is acting,* **Claire***'s trying to guess.*

Tramp I don't know any of these things!

Fliss All right, not charades.

Tramp Besides I'm so stuffed I don't think I can stand.

Fliss All right. How about . . . what's it called . . .
animal, veg . . .

Pause. A hush descends. **Fliss** *looks at* **Sid**.

No. Maybe not.

Claire, *who is over at the window comes over to whisper in*
Fliss's *ear.* **Fliss** *gets very excited, clapping her hands.*

Fliss Thank goodness. What a relief! Now I can tell you.

The **Tramp** *stares at her blankly.*

Tramp Tell me what?

Fliss I've been dying to tell you all day! (*Pause.*) Daddy –
prepare yourself for a big surprise.

Pause. He looks confused. **Fliss** *takes a deep breath.*

I didn't know whether to tell you or not, but if I had you
would've just worried all day, and you don't need to worry
because you look lovely.

Tramp Tell me what, Felicity?

Fliss We've got a special visitor today. It's all thanks to
Claire. I don't know how she did it, but she has. And I'll
have to admit I was a little worried at first, but it's what I
set out to do, so I'll just have to trust that you love me as
a daughter.

A long pause.

Tramp I don't understand.

Pause.

Fliss Daddy – meet Janis Gaines. Your wife.

Pause. Open-mouthed, the **Tramp** *stares at the tall striking woman
that glides in. And it's only after a while that we realise that we are*

looking at **Dickie**, *dragged up to the nines.*

Claire *is setting up the camera. The* **Tramp**'s *face twists to one of incomprehension.* **Janis/Dickie** *takes his/her place next to the* **Tramp**. **Claire** *comes back to the table.* **Fliss** *raises her glass.*

Fliss   I propose a toast:

Claire *and* **Dickie** *raise their glasses.*

Fliss   To Christmas. To Britain. To the Family.

Claire   To the Family.

Pause, and the **Tramp** *too raises his glass, and the camera flash goes off, freezing them there.* **Claire**, **Dickie**, **Sid** *drooling onto his chest. The* **Tramp** *stunned.*

And **Fliss**, *happy.*

End.

The Night Before Christmas

a little something for the festive season

The Night Before Christmas was first performed at the Red Room, London, on 5 December 1995. The cast was as follows:

Gary	Alan Francis
Simon	Gareth Tyrell
Elf	Michael Bettell
Cherry	Jacqueline Britt

Directed by Anthony Neilson

Characters

Gary
Simon
Elf
Cherry

A warehouse. We know because it's full of boxes. On one box lies a half-wrapped present.

Someone knocks on the door.

Long pause. They knock again.

Gary *appears, looking hyper, and runs over to the door. He opens it, revealing* **Simon**, *stamping with the cold.*

Simon This had better be fucking good, Gary.

He pulls him in, looking paranoid.

Gary Were you seen?

Simon My mother went *ape* shit, Gary. Fucking *ape*-shit.

Gary Point taken. But I think you'll agree it's worth it.

Simon Gary, you *know* what she's like! She goes to her bed at half past fucking *nine*. She gets up when it's still *dark*! It's like spending Christmas Eve in a boot camp. And she will now never shut the fuck up about this. All tomorrow there'll be tears and handwringing about how she only has me once a year and then I go out with my friends. The fact that she was asleep makes no difference. This is the level of rationality we're dealing with, do you understand? She will crush my fucking *brain* for this.

Gary I know, Si. And I feel bad. But I repeat: you wouldn't want to miss this.

Simon Miss what?

Gary All right, but first – you have to promise to keep schtum about this – until we've run it up the mast together, mater is the word, all right?

Simon In (*Checks watch.*) eight hours from now I am going to have to grin like a bastard whilst relatives I can't stomach give me aftershave, football annuals and fucking selection boxes. So I'm not making any promises, Gary. Just tell me why I'm awake in a warehouse with you when I could be at home in my cunting bed.

He lights a cigarette.

Gary   Fair enough. Wait here. Keep an eye on the door.

And **Gary** *runs off, leaving* **Simon** *standing there.*

Simon *sits down on one of the boxes that are lying around. He turns on the radio – 'A Wonderful Christmas Time' by Wings is playing. He listens to a few seconds of it, then turns it off. He picks up the half-wrapped present, takes a cursory look at it, sets it down again. Scuffling noises, and* **Gary** *re-enters with someone.* **Simon** *watches in amazement. The stranger, hands tied behind his back, would appear to be a grown man in an elf suit.*

Gary   Sit down.

The stranger does so. Long pause.

Simon   What the *fuck* – is *this*?

Gary   He's an elf.

Elf   I'm not an elf.

Gary   He calls himself a worker, but basically, he's an elf.

Long pause.

Simon   Is this meant to be funny? Am I supposed to find this funny?

Gary   I'm only telling you what he's told me.

Pause.

Simon   I'm going now, Gary. If you ever call me again, I'll have you killed.

He goes to leave.

Gary   Scout's honour, mate, if there's a deception going on, I'm not a party to it.

Simon   *If* there's a deception going on!? Have you gone completely fucking mad?!

Pause. **Gary** *looks genuine.*

Simon   What happened here exactly?

Gary   About one hour ago, I hear a noise in the storeroom. I suss it's someone removing the ventilation cover. I arm myself and go to look. I see the boy here – he doesn't see me – and I get him in a headlock. He protests that he's an elf and I get on the blower to you.

Simon   Wait, wait – there seems to have been a leap in the narrative somewhere.

Gary   Like what?

Simon   Like the bit *between* the headlock and the phone call. Like the bit where he convinces you that he's an elf and not just someone in an elf *suit*.

Gary   I'm *not* convinced. But there are things I can't explain.

Simon   Like what?

Gary   Like the size of him.

Pause.

Simon   All right, so he's a midget, so what? If he was an elf, he'd have pointy ears.

Pause.

Elf   Why?

Simon   Because that's what elves have.

Pause. **Gary** *seems quite serious.*

Are you being serious?

Pause.

If this isn't a joke, then he's a burglar or a nutcase or something, and you should call the pigs, because he's probably a serious danger to your health.

Gary   Granted, Si. Granted. This was my initial feeling. But then I asked myself: why would he be dressed as an elf?

Simon   Yes, well, that's the question, isn't it? The

question is: why would he be *dressed* as an elf? Not *is* he an elf!

Pause.

Well, I'm going to call the pigs. Where's the phone?

Elf *looks at* **Gary**.

Elf   Don't do that.

Gary   He doesn't want you to do that.

Simon   I'll bet he doesn't.

Elf   Please. I've got to get back.

Pause.

Simon   You are a bloke in an elf suit. I am calling the police, and then I am going home.

Again, **Simon** *goes to leave.*

Gary   Simon!

Simon   Gary. You haven't made an arse of me. You know that, don't you? I came because you called. The only person you're making an arse of is yourself.

Gary   It's like I said: I'm just telling you what he told me.

Pause.

Simon (*to* **Elf**)   You cheeky bastard. You must think we're a right couple of arseholes.

Gary   But that's the thing, Si. He could have said anything, so why would he say that?

Simon   Because he has contempt for us, that's why. That bastard that broke into my flat said he was looking for his pet snake! The other day there, this girl gives me a sob story about needing to get a tube home. I end up giving her one-eighty. The next day I saw her spinning the same line to some other mug. These people prey on decency. They never try it on with rich bastards, just with people like us, people that try to give someone the benefit of the doubt.

Elf Please. (*Pause.*) You don't know what you're doing keeping me here like this.

Pause. **Simon** *sits down.*

Simon All right. So you're an elf then, are you?

Elf I find the term elf insulting.

Simon What would you prefer? Gnome?

Elf I'm an employee in an International Gift Distribution Agency.

Simon Fine. So what are you doing *here*?

Elf I fell off the sledge.

Simon Of course. The sledge that you fly around on.

Elf Yes.

Simon Yes, because it's rough terrain, isn't it – the air. I mean, you need a sledge with runners, don't you? For travelling through the *air*.

Elf It's a design thing.

Gary I can buy that, Si. Speaking as a businessman.

Simon The only business you're involved in, Gary, is the back-of-a-lorry business.

Gary I resent that statement.

Simon So you were out on your sledge, which was laden with presents, I presume?

Elf In a manner of speaking.

Simon Yes, I could never figure out how you got somewhere in the region of ten million presents onto a sledge and flew halfway across the entire world without dropping any.

Gary Well, to be fair to the boy, there's probably more than one sledge in use at any given time.

Simon   Then going on my limited knowledge of sledge volume capacity, I would say you'd need approximately two billion. I find it hard to believe that two billion flying sledges would go unnoticed by radar, don't you? I mean, the sky would be like fucking Dresden.

Elf   You're being too literal.

Simon   Really.

Elf   Christmas isn't what it was.

Simon   Tell me something I don't know.

Elf   We don't do what we used to. We're a tradition, that's all.

Gary   Sort of like a Royal Family-type situation.

Simon   So what do you do now?

Elf   Eat biscuits and drink glasses of milk. (*Pause.*) I don't always drink the milk actually. There's often a thin film of scum across the top.

Gary *makes a disgusted face.*

Simon   So you come down the chimney to get the milk and biscuits . . . ?

Elf   Obviously, chimneys are not always practical. We often have to jimmy the back door.

Gary   Hence the toolbag.

Elf   That's right.

Simon   He has a *toolbag*?

Gary   He's never denied breaking and entering, to be fair.

Simon (*shakes head*)   This is insane.

Gary   So you don't deliver presents?

Elf   We never really did. Not in the way you mean.

Pause.

Could you at least undo my hands?

Gary *goes to do so.*

Simon Not a *chance.*

Gary *stops,* **Simon** *glaring at him.*

Elf We've been doing this for a long time. And back when we started, the presents children got were very basic. All we did was enhance them. We made the apples shinier. We made the books smell better. And not just the presents either. We could enhance the rooms too – make the windows brighter, the beds higher. Alter smells and sounds. What we brought wasn't a solid thing. It was a gift of perception. Everything was fine until the Plastic age.

Gary What was that then?

Elf That was when you started to mass produce gifts made of synthetic materials. Plastic is very hard to enhance, you see. You can make it smell a bit better but that's about it.

Simon This is fascinating. Absolute fucking drivel, but fascinating.

Elf No, think about it – did you never get a present in a big box – a present you really wanted – and you'd take it out and look at it for a while, only to find yourself compulsively drawn back to the box?

Gary I did. I remember. A spacesuit it was. Threw it away and played in the box all day.

Elf Right. And that box could be anything, couldn't it? It could be a spaceship, or a car, or a house.

Gary It was a bloody fascinating box.

Elf That's because cardboard is an organic product, and they're much easier to enhance. The gift itself hadn't been enhanced. The box had.

Simon   So how do you do that?

The **Elf** *shakes his head a bit, looking pained for a second.*

Elf   I'm sorry?

Simon   How do you enhance these organic substances?

Elf   I'm really not supposed to talk about it.

Simon   Look, the only thing that's stopping me calling the police is that I'm fascinated to hear what shit you talk next.

Gary   So make like *Jackanory*, or it's the cop shop for you.

Gary *is doing his best to look threatening.*

Elf (*sighs*)   We use a very fine powder, that we sprinkle around the child, who ingests it through the pores and airways.

Pause.

Gary   Drugs?

Elf   That would be the easiest way for you to understand it, yes.

Simon   You're telling us that the Christmas feeling is a drug?

Elf   Yes. But the lightest, most benign drug in existence.

Gary   With no side effects?

Elf   We did find that we were using so much of it that it tended to permeate the air. The only undesirable effect is that it causes a stimulant effect in young children, keeping them awake a bit longer than usual.

Gary   What's the dosage?

Elf   A few grains.

Gary   And are you presently in possession?

Elf (*pause*)   No, it's very tightly rationed. Listen, please, you have to let me go now. Everybody will be very worried.

Gary Simon – did you hear that? The Christmas feeling in powdered form.

Simon Yes.

Gary Small dosages, no side effects. That could be a nice little earner.

Simon But he doesn't have any with him.

Gary Even so, I reckon it's a square deal. We give you your boy, you give us a spot of the old Yuletide gear.

Simon Yes, but he says he hasn't – (*Pause.*) – what the fuck are you talking about?! You actually believe he's an elf! Don't you?!

Gary No, that's unfair. The jury is still out.

Simon The fact that they're even deliberating is a sign that you are seriously mentally ill.

Gary Keep up the Q and A, see if he squeaks.

Pause.

Simon All right. So. I'm still wondering how you manage to get round all these houses in one night.

Elf We have a completely different concept of time to you. Our hearts beat much slower than yours. Your minutes are like our days. You never see us because we move too fast. That's what I'm saying: I've been sitting in this chair for about a fortnight in your time.

Gary *puts his hand on the* **Elf***'s chest, and looks at his watch.*

Gary One.

A long pause.
And then some more.

Two (*Pause.*) It's a damn slow heartbeat, Si.

Simon *comes over, puts his hand on the* **Elf***'s chest.*

Simon   One.

A long pause.
And then some more.

Two – you're holding your breath!

Elf   I'm not.

Simon   There's guys that can slow their heartbeats down.
People can do all sorts of things.

Pause.

I'll bet you're having a good fucking laugh. Thinking
you've made fools of us because we're listening to you. But
we're listening to you because we're nice guys. You'd've
broken into another storeroom they'd have kicked the shit
out of you.

Elf   I know you're nice.

Simon   And that's what you're playing on.
And then we don't call the police and we let you go and
you have a good laugh at our expense.

Gary *is on his mobile.*

Gary   Lulu?
I know, I'm sorry – something came up. So what's the
story?

Long pause.

So I won't see you tomorrow . . . ? But what about his
present?
What, *now*?
Well, I . . .
(*Sighs.*) All right. Yeah. All right.
Bollocks. The wife's coming over. We better get this sorted.

Simon   But I'm sure she'll be *thrilled* to meet a real-life
elf.

Gary   Don't know about that, Si. Not much of the little
girl left in Lulu.

Simon   So what about Santa then? He's out there tonight, is he?

Pause.

Elf   No. He's old now. He doesn't come out with us.

Simon   Where's he then? The North Pole?

Elf   That wouldn't be very practical, would it?

Simon   So where do you stay?

Elf   Hartlepool.

Simon   Hartlepool?!

Elf   The British branch, yes. Although, again, I'm trying to make it easy for you. In actual fact, we simply exist in the space that you would call Hartlepool. How much longer are you going to keep me here?

Simon   Until you tell me the truth.

Elf   I don't lie.

Simon   You're not making a fool out of me. I'll let people take advantage of my good nature up to a point, but this is where I draw the line.

Elf   But you don't understand . . .

Simon   I get swindled every day. By the bank, by the boss, by shopkeepers, and beggars and dealers and so-called friends –

Elf   I *can't* lie . . .

Simon   But this is where I draw the line. I draw the line at fucking elves. You admit that you're a burglar, maybe we'll let you go.

Elf   But I physically *can't* lie. So I won't be able to tell you what you want to hear, and you'll never let me go, and they'll be looking for me. They won't risk me falling into human hands. They'll call off Christmas if they have to. It'll be ruined for thousands of children.

Gary   That sounds a bit hectic, Si. Christmas ruined for thousands of children. That's bordering on the Vaderesque.

Simon   Well, they might as well get a taste of things to come.

Pause.

That's the side effect of your fucking powder. A lifetime of the DTs. Every year the same question: is it me that's changed, or is it Christmas? Is it Christmas that's changed or is it me? What have I lost? What have I gained? Will I make it to the next one? Every Christmas just another door open on the advent calendar to death. And what's behind the doors? Great revelations? Shining moments of truth? No. Shitty little drawings of kettles.

Pause.

So the little brats can fucking lump it for a year. It's not your poxy powder that keeps them awake at night, it's greed, their little hearts pumping with greed, their eyes shiny with it, totting up the prices of the crap on their lists. We're blooding them that's all, it's the same thing as these bastards that wipe foxblood on their kids' faces, we're blooding them into the capitalist world. The way they sit in hordes and devour adverts, like dingoes at a kill. Your powder's just the sugar on the pill.

Gary   Have to put in a word for the old festive season there, Si. You're giving it maximum Scrooge. It's not so bad.

Simon   I wonder if your enthusiasm could have anything to do with the contents of these fucking boxes? I'll bet you've made a few quid this year.

Elf   Or maybe he has a child?

Pause.

Gary   Have as a matter of fact.

*He takes wallet out of his pocket, shows the picture to the **Elf**.*

Andrew Paul Nutsinger, age five. The Paul is a tribute to the boy Weller, ex-Jam and Style Council frontman and now currently enjoying renewed success with a string of hit albums. (*Pause.*) Terribly runny shit though. (*Pause.*) Got his present there. That's why his mum's coming over. Like to give him it myself, but they're spending tomorrow at his Gran's and things are a bit frosty between us. You know.

Elf   You're separated from your wife?

Gary (*pause*)   Wasn't much good at the husband business. I was getting better, but I suppose she got tired of waiting. I'm better at the father bit, when I get a chance.

Pause.

Elf   He's a nice-looking boy.

Gary *puts his wallet away.*

Gary   That's my business.

Elf   But you see, anyone who has children in the house is bound to breathe some of the powder in. You can't help it.

Simon   What about the people who don't have children? Not everyone can have children, you know. We never get the feeling again, is that it?

Elf   There are children everywhere.

Simon   Balls. You can't even smile at a child nowadays without someone calling you a pervert. Anyway, I don't want a sniff of hand-me-down joy. I want a faceful of the fucking stuff.

Gary   Amen to that.

Simon   You give us a blast of the Christmas feeling, and then we'll believe you. Do that for us, and we'll let you go.

Pause.

Elf   Even if I had any, I couldn't.

Simon   Why the fuck not?

Pause.

Elf   Because you're dirtyboys.

Pause.

Simon   We're what?

Elf   You're dirtyboys.

Gary   Dirtyboys?

Elf (*pause*)   You've done the filthybusiness.

Simon   The filthybusiness?

He looks at **Gary**.

Gary   I think he means sex.

Pause.

Simon   We're not allowed the Christmas feeling because we've had sex?

Elf   It's not that you're not allowed it, it's just that after you've – done the filthybusiness – it takes a lot more powder to achieve the same effect. It wouldn't be viable.

Gary   Viable. As a businessman, I can see it. But it seems a bit harsh.

Simon   It's a fucking outrage!

Gary   It is something of a Catch 22 situation. Considering that we've got to sow our Quakers in order to further the species and make more kids to enjoy Christmas, it seems a bit unjust to give us the bum's rush as a reward.

Elf   I don't make the rules.

Simon   That's all we need – a fucking jobsworth elf.

Gary   Shitcakes.

Simon   That's it, you see: the child is innocent, therefore the adult must be guilty. Guilty of the most natural thing in the world. How the fuck did that happen? What the fuck has the Christmas feeling got to do with sex?

What about children who've been *forced* to do the filthybusiness? Little abused children? Do they get the Christmas feeling?

Pause.

Elf No. No Christmas feeling for them.

Pause. **Gary** *and* **Simon** *are gutted.*

I don't make the rules.

Miserable. They sit down. A long pause.

Gary I must say, though, I have noticed that Yuletide is peak time for matters of a heartbreaking nature.
Lulu left me just before Christmas '93.
It was snowing when she drove off.
(*Smiles fondly.*) We had an awful time getting the car to start.

Pause.

Simon *looks at his watch.*

Simon I'm tired of this. I'm going to call the police.

Pause.

Is everything in here legal?

Gary Mostly.

Simon Only mostly?

Gary Yeah, but it's cool. Third of my customers are bizzies.

Simon *indicates* **Gary***'s mobile.* **Gary** *gives it to him, and* **Simon** *dials 999. Pause. The* **Elf** *looks distressed.*

Elf (*shakes head*) You don't know what you're doing.

Simon Police please.
Yes, I'd like to report an attempted burglary.
Yes, we have the criminal on the premises.
No. No.

Pause. He looks at **Gary**.

Gary   Pricebreaker Warehouse, Stroud Green Road.

Simon   Pricebreaker Warehouse, Stroud Green Road.

Pause.

Gary's place, yes.
My name is Simon. Templer.
T-E-M-P-L-*E*-R.
No, it's not a joke.
Yes, I know.
All right. Thanks.

He turns off the mobile.

Well. That's that. They're on their way.

Pause. The **Elf** *is looking unwell.*

All you had to do was tell the truth. You brought it on
yourself. But you're not making fools of us. Christmas or
no Christmas.

Pause.

Gary   Have to admit though: it was a good story.

Simon   Yes, well maybe he should give up trying to rip
people off and go into chidren's novels.

And then there is a knock at the door.

Pause. They all look at each other.

Simon   That was quick.

Gary   It might be Lulu.

Pause.

I'll go and see. Keep the noise down.

Pause. Off he goes to look.

Simon *left with the* **Elf**.

Elf   Please, let me go. Just undo me, I can still get away.

Simon *says nothing.*

Elf You don't understand. We get sick if we're away too long. I'm starting to feel bad now. Please.

Simon What's your name?

Elf Call me what you like, just please let me go.

Simon Tell me your name.

Elf It would take you fifteen minutes to *say* my name.

Simon Are you ill?

Elf I feel very bad.

Simon I mean mentally.

Elf I feel dizzy.

Arguing going on outside.

Cherry (*offstage*) . . . no, you owe me! You *owe* me, you fucking weasel!

Gary (*offstage*) Cherry – listen – I'll sort – I'll sort you out – tomorrow –

The arguments burst into the room, in the flamboyant shape of **Cherry**.

Cherry You'll sort me out right fucking now, you cheap fucking spiv. You owe me some shit and I'm here to collect.

She sees the other two.

Well fucking well, what's the story here? A tied-up midget and a wanker in his PJs. And I thought I'd seen it all.

Gary *looks embarrassed.*

Gary Cherry, this is Si, an old friend. Si – Cherry. Sort of a – personal assistant.

Cherry Yeah. I take down anything he says.

Simon *just stares at her.*

Cherry (*pause*) Who's the Boy Wonder?

Simon He's an employee of an International Gift Distribution Agency.

Cherry In English.

Simon An elf.

Cherry Yeah. I've been Santa's little helper a few times myself. (*To* **Gary**.) Now where's the stuff you owe me, speedbump?

Gary Turn it down, Cherry. We don't want any trouble, do we?

Cherry The *crap* – or I start doing the Shake'n'Vac.

She is obviously referring to some sexual practice. **Gary** *starts looking through the boxes.*

Gary One of these, it's one of these. Just give me a mo.

Pause. **Cherry** *looks at* **Simon** *and the* **Elf**. *She shakes her head.*

Cherry You're a sorry-looking pair of monkeys.

Simon And what the fuck are you?

Cherry I'm a Bond girl.

Simon Is that what they call scrubbers now?

Cherry Button your lip, or I'll use it for wrapping-paper.

Simon He really is an elf.

Cherry Yeah, and I'm Snow White.

Simon Is that rhyming slang?

Cherry Fuck you with sage and onion stuffing.

Gary *has found the toys.*

Gary Here we go, here we go – toys for the boys.

He hands them over.

Two Power Rangers, Biker Mouse and I'll throw in an

ugly ball free. Now, Cherry, I'd appreciate it if you'd (leave us to what we're –)

Cherry (*pause*)   What the fuck's this?

She holds up a packet. Pause. **Gary** *looks at it.*

This isn't a Power Ranger . . .

Gary   What is it?

Cherry   It's an Electric Warrior.

Gary (*pause*)   It's as near-as-damnit.

Cherry   Well, it's not fucking near *enough*.

Gary   Cherry, now – that's what I meant. Electric Warrior, Power Ranger, what's the difference?

Cherry   This is no use to me! Do you understand? I said to my boy he'd have what he wanted, and what he wanted is Power Rangers. This is no fucking *use* to me!

Gary   Cherry. What can I do? This is all I've got.

Cherry   This is cheap, plastic shite! It's a cheap imitation! Do you understand?!

She smacks him on the head with the packet.

A Biker Mouse for your cock and a Power Ranger apiece for your saggy balls, that was the deal.

Gary   Saggy?!

Cherry (*to* **Simon** *and the* **Elf**)   I do the good ship lollipop on this freak twice a week and he palms me off with imitation crap!

Gary *feigns confusion to* **Simon** *and the* **Elf**. **Cherry** *kicks him up the arse. This gets his attention.*

Cherry   See, my boy goes to school with crap like this, the other ones laugh at him. They say his mum's cheap, they make him feel like a fool. Well, it's not going to happen. You're going to give me my due, and I'm staying here until you do.

Gary   Cherry – have mercy – I've got an ex-wife on the way round scenario!

Cherry   Boo fucking hoo. Cross my palm with Power Rangers and I'll be gone.

Simon   The police are on their way. They'll deal with both of them.

Cherry   Get a life. I've fucked half the Met whilst the other half watched. And I'm sure I could tell them a few interesting things about Gary Nutsinger.

Gary   Now look – let's all calm down. It's Christmas.

Pause.

Cherry, I've got some dosh now – let me give you the money.

Cherry   Get it through your brain, footface. My kid wakes up in a few hours. Money's no good to me.

Gary   Well, where am I going to get Power Rangers at this time of night?

Cherry   Dig a tunnel under Hamley's, I don't give a fuck. It's your problem.

Elf   Please – you have to let me go. It's not too late to save Christmas.

Cherry   What the *fuck's* going on here anyway?

Gary   We told you – he's an elf.

Cherry   What are they doing to you?

Simon   We caught him breaking in. He insists that he's an elf.

Cherry   Does he now?

Pause.

So you're to blame for all this then?

Elf   For what?

Cherry For fucking Christmas!
Do you know how many extra cocks I've had to suck for
this bullshit?
How many extra shags and handjobs? Running around like
a blue-arsed fly: shops, shag, shops, shag.
Do you have any idea what a fucking pain it is?

(*To* **Simon**.) Give us a fag.

Simon What do you say?

Brutally, she twists his nipple.

Cherry Give us a fag!

He complies. She doesn't have to ask for a light.

As if things weren't bad enough. The gas, the rent, the
council tax, the electricity, the phone, the fines and you
think things can't get any worse and then suddenly it's
fucking Christmas. And he wants this and he wants that.
This year he wanted some computer thing – hundred and
fifty fucking quid. And it's only a small thing so it's not like
you could just give him *that* – there'd have to be other stuff
too. (*Pause.*) You watch the kids' programmes on Saturday
morning. If it was the Russians doing it they'd call it
Brainwashing.

Simon Exactly.

Cherry A break every ten minutes, six adverts every
break, for three hours. One piece of crap after another,
and down in the corner, in tiny letters, the price. Devious
fucking bastards.
(*To* **Elf**.) So you're to blame for all that are you, shortarse?

Elf I'm just an employee . . .

Simon *warms to this.*

Simon Oh no. If you want to be an elf, you'll take the
blame. You'll take the blame for all of it – the Queen's
speech, the *Radio Times* Bumper Edition, the Christmas
Number One, every miserable cheesy facet of it. Christmas
crackers full of shite, with little cardboard bits that don't

bang. Cheap Christmas cards with pictures of silver fucking balls on the front.

Cherry A twenty-five per cent rise in suicides.

Simon Trees that piss pine needles all over the floor. Those crap chocolate Santas you hang on them.

Cherry I say we torture the little fucker.

Simon I completely concur.

Elf No – please – !

Gary Now hang on . . .

Cherry Make him eat fruitcake until he dies.

Simon Sit him in a room for five hours with a pensioner in a V-neck.

Gary This is a bit harsh. I thought we didn't think he *was* an elf.

Cherry I don't give a toss if he is or not. I just want some fucker to blame.

Elf Please – it's not my fault!

Simon *He's* the one that *insists* he's an elf.

Gary You're frightening him . . .

Simon Good.

Gary He really doesn't look very well, Si.

Cherry Maybe he wants a cigarette.

She presses her cigarette to the **Elf***'s mouth. The* **Elf** *struggles.*

Come on – take a drag.

Simon *squeezes the* **Elf***'s nose shut.*

Gary Stop it –

Involuntarily, the **Elf** *takes a drag. He coughs his guts up.* **Cherry** *and* **Simon** *are amused.* **Gary** *pushes them away.*

Cherry   There you go – proof that smoking can seriously damage your elf.

Gary *steps between them and the* **Elf**.

Gary   Leave him alone, you sick bastards. This is how Fred and Rosemary West started, doing things like that.

Simon   He's a sanctimonious little turd. (*To* **Cherry**.) He told us that if you've had sex, you can't get the Christmas feeling. Can you believe that? Only virgins get the Christmas feeling.

Cherry   Yeah, well they're fucking welcome to it.

Gary   Look, we've called the rozzers. They'll deal with him.

Simon   If they ever arrive. If we'd been calling from fucking Hampstead they'd be here soon enough.

Elf   Please – let me go – .

Gary   We can't, mate. Not now.

Elf   It's not my fault what you've done to Christmas!

The **Elf** *doubles up in pain.*

Gary   Christ, what's wrong with him?

Simon   Nothing's wrong with him.

Gary *is kneeling down by the* **Elf**.

Gary   Looks authentic to me.

Elf   Please – I'm sick – we get – sick –

Gary   He did say that – he said they get sick if they're away too long.

Simon   The only thing that's making him sick is the thought of a night in the fucking cells!

The **Elf** *contorts in pain.*

Gary   I'm finding this distressing.

Simon　He's acting.

Cherry　No he's not.

Gary　Maybe we should call an ambulance.

Cherry　That's not what he needs.

Gary　Suddenly you're an expert on elf anatomy?

Simon　Maybe this is all a bizarre dream. Really I'm at home asleep.

Cherry　Look at his arms.

Gary　What?

Cherry　Roll up the sleeves and look at his fucking arms.

Pause. **Gary** *does so. He sees.*

Cherry　Trackmarks.

Pause.

Gary　What does this mean?

Simon　It means that our elf is a junkie.

Cherry　Mystery solved, I reckon.

Gary　So why did he break in here?

Simon　So he could steal something to sell for money. Or swap it for some of whatever he's on.

Gary　What, like smack or something?

Pause. To **Elf***:*

Is that right? Are you some sort of junkie?

Pause. The **Elf** *nods.*

Gary　You need some smack?

The **Elf** *shakes his head.*

Cherry　Sulph, is it?

Elf (*pained*)　Christmas . . .

Gary   Christmas?

Elf (*pause*)   ... Feeling ...

Pause.

Gary   Christmas Feeling?

Pause.

Bugger me – he's addicted to the Christmas Feeling powder! He's been banging up the magic powder!

Simon   He doesn't give up, does he?

Cherry   What the fuck are you talking about – magic powder?

Gary   It's a long story.

Cherry   Is this some kind of a wind-up?

Simultaneously:

Gary   No.

Simon   Yes.

Pause.

Cherry   Look, I just want the fucking Power Rangers, Gary. I've got a babysitter waiting to go home. I don't have time for this bollocks.

*The **Elf**'s pain seems to be passing.*

Gary   Are you all right?

*Pause. The **Elf** nods.*

Elf   It comes and goes.

Gary   So it'll come back?

Elf (*nods*)   Worse.

Gary   How much worse?

Elf   Much. If I don't get back to the sledge.

Pause.

Gary   I don't like this. I don't want a dead elf on my conscience. We should let him go.

Cherry   Why don't you just let him go anyway, you couple of stool-pigeons. What good's a night in the cells going to do him, elf or not?

Simon   'Elf or not?'! (*Pause.*) Am I the only sane person in this room?

Cherry   No, you're the only total fucking arse.

Simon   This bloke tells us he's an elf. He says elves live in Hartlepool, and that the Christmas feeling is a narcotic powder. Now he's telling us that he's addicted to it.

Elf   We *all* are.

Gary   What – all the elves?

The **Elf** *nods.*

Pause. **Simon** *laughs, shakes his head, at a loss for words.*

Gary   Santa's little helpers? Junkies?! That's terrible!

Gary *looks at* **Cherry**. *She says nothing.*

Simon   So now Santa's a drug dealer, is he? What next – Captain Bird's Eye is a paedophile with a slave boat? Mr Benn was a serial rapist?

Gary   Is that right? Santa's a pusher?

Elf (*pause*)   He doesn't know anything about it. Please don't tell him, it'll break his heart!

Simon   He's missed that, has he? That his entire workforce is on the pixie dust?

Cherry   You know, I'm fucking *sick* of the sound of your voice, mate.

Simon (*pause*)   Of *my* voice?

Gary   Have to say it, Si – you *are* giving out an unhelpful vibe.

Simon   What about *her*?! She was all for torturing him! (*He points at* **Cherry**.)

Cherry   I was only fucking about.

Simon   What are you saying? That he's what he says he is?

Cherry   Who the fuck knows? But maybe *he* thinks he's what he says he is, d'you ever think of that? You either go with it or you don't.

Simon   Well, I *don't*.

Cherry   Right. So your point is noted, so shut the fuck up.

Simon *looks at* **Gary**.

Simon   Is that what you think I should do? Shut the fuck up?

Gary (*pause*)   No, I just think . . . we should hear his story.

Pause. **Simon** *sits down, with a sigh.*

Simon   You're not going to hear anything, because the police are going to get here any minute.

Elf   You have to let me go. Please. If they lock me up, I'll never get back to the sledge.

Pause. **Gary** *looks at* **Cherry**, *who shrugs.*

Simon   You let him go, he'll have made pricks of us all.

Pause.

Elf   I can make it worth your while.

Pause.

Gary   How?

Elf (*pause*)   I can grant you each a wish.

Pause. **Simon** *shakes his head.*

Gary   What do you mean, a wish?

Elf   If you let me go, I can grant you each one wish.

Simon   You'll be in touch, will you?

Gary   Yeah, I mean, if we let you go, how do we know you'll do what you say?

Elf   Because I don't lie.

Simon *snorts.*

Gary   The wishes first, and then we'll let you go.

Pause.

Elf   All right, but tell the police not to come. (*Pause.*) If I don't do what I say, you can call them again.

Pause.

Gary   That sounds fair enough.

Pause. He looks at the others. Again, **Simon** *shakes his head.*

Cherry   This should be interesting.

Gary *dials a number.*

Gary   Police.
Hi – we reported an attempted break-in – is that Deniece?
Deniece, it's Gary from Pricebreakers –
Not too bad, yourself?
Yeah. Well, look, we don't need that car –
No, it was just a . . . misunderstanding –
Yeah. That sort of thing. It's sorted.
Ask away. Nephews, right.
Yeah, sort of.
Well, they're not exactly Power Rangers, but they're bloody close.
I can do you a Hungry Hippo, no bother. Usually retails at thirty, but for you, I'll do it for ten.
Well, give us a bell. All right. Have a nice one.

Puts phone away.

All right. Done.

Pause.

Elf   Then tell me what you wish for.

Simon   I wish I had some more fags.

Elf   Granted. There's some in that toolbag.

Pause. **Gary** *goes over and looks in the toolbag. He brings out a packet of cigarettes.*

Gary   Bugger me, Si!

Simon   What does that prove?! That he's got a packet of fags in his bag?!

Gary   I didn't see them last time I looked. And they're your brand as well.

Cherry   And we know he doesn't smoke, does he?

Gary   Have to admit, it's a bit *X-File*-esque.

Pause.

Simon   Well, that wasn't my wish anyway.

Gary *throws* **Simon** *the cigarettes. He jumps away as if they carry the plague.*

Simon   I don't want them – that wasn't my wish.

Elf   I can only grant you one each. As soon as the wish is spoken, there's no going back.

Simon   All you did was give me a packet of fags out your bag!

Elf   That was what you wished for.

Simon   It was an offhand comment, I didn't know it was my actual wish!

Cherry   You think it's all shit anyway.

Simon   Yes, but that still wasn't what my wish would have been! I mean – I would have said a wish that would have been harder for him to do.

Cherry Well, we've learnt from your mistake then, haven't we?

Simon That's not fair! That wasn't my wish!

Elf Please, we have to hurry.

Simon This is a fucking con!

Gary Is there anything we can't wish for?

Elf Tell me your wish. If I can't do it, you can have another one.

Simon How's that then? How come they can say what they wish for, and then get another one?

Cherry You wished for cigarettes, he gave you some.

Simon That wasn't a real wish! You all know that – it was just something I said, 'I wish I had some fags'!

Cherry Don't be such a fucking brat.

Simon That's easy for you to say, you've still got a wish.

Gary Here, Cherry, you can wish for those Power Rangers.

Cherry I'm not using my wish for fucking Power Rangers! You can use *your* wish for Power Rangers.

Gary It's you that wants them, not me.

Cherry It's *you* that owes *me* the Power Rangers, so *you* can use *your* wish.

Gary You must be joking.

Cherry What? (*Pause.*) That's fair.

Gary (*pause*) You can't ask me to use my wish for *that* . . .

Cherry All I'm saying, Gary, is that I want those Power Rangers. I don't care how you get them, but you better fucking get them. At the moment, I'm just looking forward to meeting your ex-wife. I'm sure she's heard all about me.

She makes an odd gesture that would seem to signify water cascading down her face. Whatever it might mean, it mortifies **Gary**.

Gary (*to* **Simon**)   I can't believe she's threatening me like that . . .

Simon   Have to say, it seems fair enough – *mate*.

Gary   Oh, cheers.

Simon   Just returning the compliment.

Pause.

Gary   Look, Cherry – I mean, what are you going to wish for? Probably something big, right? Probably something that'll benefit your kid in some way?

Cherry (*shrugs*)   I don't know yet.

Gary   Well, you can't deny me the chance to do the same.

The **Elf** *doubles with pain.*

Simon   Doesn't look like either of you'll be getting any wishes at this rate.

Gary *goes to the* **Elf**.

Gary   Is it worse?

The **Elf** *nods.*

Gary   Much?

Elf   A bit . . . you have to . . . hurry up . . . or I'll be too weak to . . . grant your wishes . . .

Gary *waits for the* **Elf** *to recover from this latest wave.*

Elf   I'm all right. Just – please – make your wishes.

Simon   I can think of a few, if you're stuck.

Cherry   We're not.

Gary   All right, all right – I wish . . .

Cherry   That I had the Power Rangers for Cherry.

Gary No! That's not what I wish! Does that count?

The **Elf** *shakes his head.* **Cherry** *laughs.*

Gary That's bloody lucky for you, Cherry!
It's not funny. That wouldn't have been my wish, if it had counted. It would have been yours.

Simon Now you see how it feels?!

Cherry I wish you'd –

Gary *clamps his hand over her mouth. Pause, and then he releases her.*

Cherry Thanks. (*Pause.*) I'd appreciate it if you would stop going on. You had your chance, and you fucking blew it. I am trying to think.

Simon An effort, is it?

Gary You see we have to be very careful how we word our wishes.

Cherry Like what?

Gary Well, for instance – I might say that I ... desired that my wife would not arrive here and find me with you – a scrubber.

Cherry Or you could phone her up instead.

Gary I couldn't, actually. But even so, I've no intention of wasting my wish on something so petty. But if I *did*, I could find that my ... desire came true in an undesirable manner – like, for instance, she might not arrive because she had been killed in a terrible road accident.

Cherry That's a good point.

Gary Or I might say that I desired to be a millionaire. But I could just as easily say that I desired to be the richest man in the world, or that I desired for *everyone* in the world to be a millionaire.

Cherry But if everyone was a millionaire, the price of everything would go up anyway and you'd be back at square one.

Simon   How about if just the three of us were millionaires? You could wish that all three of us were millionaires, and then *you* could wish for something else for all three of us. That would maximise our wishes.

Gary   Sort of like being at a Chinese restaurant and sharing courses.

Cherry   What, and you'd share out your fags, yeah?

Pause. **Simon** *simmers.*

Simon   Look, you learnt a valuable lesson from my experience, and it's helping you to choose more wisely now.

Gary   Of course, we could be more general. Less selfish. We could wish for a state of never-ending peace in the world.

Cherry   Yeah. That's true. A safe and peaceful world for our kids to grow up in.

Simon   Or one of you could wish that, and the other one could wish that all three of us were fucking loaded.

Gary   I thought you were against all that capitalist stuff.

Simon   Yes, because I'm skint!

Cherry   There's so many things you could wish for . . .

Pause.

Elf (*in pain*)   Please . . .

Gary   All right, mate, we'll be with you shortly.

Simon   I know – you could each wish for another ten wishes.

Gary   Is that allowed?

The **Elf** *shakes his head.*

Gary   Not allowed. Good one though, Si.

Cherry   Time. You could wish for time.

Gary   You might end up with a Rolex.

Cherry   No, I mean you could wish to live for ever.

Gary   Like in *Highlander*. Mind you, he ended up with some bloke chasing him round trying to cut his head off.

Pause.

Simon   It'd be fucking awful anyway, living for ever. Seeing everyone die.

Gary   And you could live to be a hundred, really wrinkly and shitting your pants and such, and then just go on like that for ever.

Cherry   But time – it wouldn't have to be living for ever. It could be having some time back. Having some time back so you could undo a wrong decision. Or having some time back with someone – that you lost. Or something.

Gary   Yeah. (*Pause.*) I wouldn't mind seeing my old man again. Mum'd like that too. That'd make Christmas like Christmas again. The stink of my dad's feet mixing with the smell of roast turkey. (*Pause.*) But it's a bit creepy that, wishing someone dead would come back. They might come back a zombie, like in *Pet Sematary*. Neighbours'd think you'd forgotten to put the bins out.

Cherry   I didn't mean it had to be someone dead. You could spend a day with someone that you used to . . . go out with, or something.

Simon   But then the day would end. Just be a memory again.

Gary   Really you mean that you could wish that someone who used to love you would love you again.

Pause.

Cherry   Yeah. Maybe you're right.

Gary   So who are you thinking of, Cherry?

Cherry None of your business, is it?

Pause. **Gary** *shrugs. Pause.*

My kid's dad is who I'm thinking of.

Simon What is this, the fucking Absent Fathers' Society?

Gary Don't you see him ever?

Cherry (*pause*) Nah. Not really. (*Pause.*) Don't suppose I even liked him that much, when I think about it. He was a fucking tosser. But it'd be nice for Matthew – to have a family, you know. (*Pause.*) I used to work from home, yeah? I'd have five or six tricks back a night. And one day he asked me which one was daddy. None of them, I said. Are you *trying* to find daddy, he asks. (*Pause.*) All the time, I said. All the fucking time. Worked the street ever since. Boo fucking hoo, Cherry. So fucking what. But it's what you were saying: it'd make Christmas feel like Christmas again. Cos however much you hated it, you knew where you were when you were part of a family. Sometimes it'd be nice to know where you were for a while. (*Pause.*) Anyway – Boo fucking hoo.

Gary Aladdin never had these problems, did he? (*Pause.*) It's a matter of figuring out what's most important to you right now. That shouldn't be hard.
Cherry – what's most important to you? Right now?

Cherry Like I said, my little boy.

Gary You want him to have a family?

Cherry I want him to have a good life.

Gary So that's what you should wish for, isn't it?

Cherry And I do, every day.

Gary Yeah, but this time, it's an elf that's giving you the wish.

Simon I'm sorry but this is such shit. The future. Families. A good life. I mean you could find him a father tomorrow, and he could turn out to be a violent alcoholic or a child abuser or God knows what. The fact is you can't wish a future. The best thing you could do for your kid is stop being a tart and get a proper fucking job! And if you want to make him happy, if you want to make him smile, wish for the fucking Power Rangers, because tomorrow morning's about as far in the future as happiness gets.

Cherry   You're a fucking tosser, mate, you know that? Where do you get the right to say any of that to me?

Simon   Then ignore me. Wish that your child has a good life, and then you won't have to make any effort, will you? You sad bastard. I mean, what d'you think's going to happen – you'll go home and find him lying in a Jacuzzi with servant girls feeding him grapes? I don't think so. I think everything'll be exactly the same as it was when you left. So what are you going to do then? How long will it take until you realise you've been made a total arse of? Take my advice. Wish for the Power Rangers.

Cherry   Piss off.

Simon   Wish for the Power Rangers, and then we'll know if our friend here's telling the truth. If he is, then Gary can wish for all of us.

Pause.

Gary   Why not?

Pause. She takes a deep breath.

Cherry   I wish I had some Power Rangers for my son.

*The **Elf** nods.*

Elf (*in pain*)   Granted.

Long pause.

Cherry   So where are they?

Elf   I haven't got them just now.

Simon   Well, there's a surprise.

Elf I said I could grant you . . . a wish. I didn't say . . . I could transport things . . . through space.

Gary He didn't, to be fair.

Cherry But I need them *now*.

Pause.

What a fucking swizz!

Simon Then it looks like it's up to me.

*They all look at **Simon**, who wanders over to the present that **Gary** has been wrapping throughout the play. He tosses it to **Cherry**.*

Granted.

Gary Now hold on a minute – !

*Pause. She unwraps it, to reveal a Power Rangers set. She looks at **Gary**. He looks guilty. Pause.*

What?

Cherry You've had these all the time?

Pause.

Gary Look, they're bloody hard to get hold of.

Cherry Certainly a lot scarcer than prostitutes, that's for sure!

Gary Cherry, those are for my son. I can't let you have them.

Simon For fuck's sake, Gary – the kid's got no father and a tart for a mother. You're not even seeing Andrew until Boxing Day.

Gary You're out of order here, Si. Lulu's going to be here any minute. D'you know what she'll be like if I haven't got him anything?

Simon What are you worried about? That your kid will be heartbroken? That she'll never let you see him again?

Gary   No, that she'll break all my teeth and tie a knot in my throat!

Simon   She's five foot one!

Gary   Mike Tyson's not that tall either.

Pause.

Si, you don't understand. She thinks I'm a good-for-nothing bastard.

Simon   Acute perception is her best quality.

Gary   I'm not joking, Si. (*Pause.*) All through the marriage she used to tell me that I was cold and selfish, that I only ever thought about myself. That I couldn't look after a rubber plant, never mind a child.

Simon   Why do you care what she says?

Gary   Because she's my wife.

Simon   Your ex-wife.

Gary   Yes, my *ex*-wife.

Simon   So why do you care what she thinks? She left you, she took the kid, she's living with someone else, why do you care what she thinks?

Cherry   Because he loves her, you tit.

Gary   No great revelation there, Si. Most husbands love their ex-wives.

Simon   But do most ex-wives love their husbands?

Gary   High probability of it, but I'm no expert.

Pause.

See that's the problem: I used to think a marriage broke up because the couple concerned were no longer in love. But you might as well believe in Santa. Love's a grotto, mate, and Eros wears a false beard and smells of whisky.

Pause.

Simon That's the worst analogy I've ever heard.

Gary I'm working on it.

Simon You want her back, don't you? Lulu?

Pause.

Gary No. Not really. I mean – now and then I wonder. What might have happened. I really thought I was getting there. That we might have been happy. Eventually. Maybe. But not really. I mean, she loves someone else now. So no.

Pause.

Yes.

Simon Yes?

Gary Yes. I do. More than anything. If I'm being honest. But it's not an option.

Simon Not if she finds Cherry here anyway.

Gary No.

Simon So give her the Power Rangers.

Pause. He gives **Cherry** *the Power Rangers.*

Gary Merry ⹂ristmas, Cherry.

Pause. Softly, **Cherry** *kisses him on the cheek.*

Cherry Merry Christmas.

Pause.

Gary Thanks for all the wanks an' that.

Cherry Pleasure.

Simon Aw. How fucking sweet. And now you know what to wish for.

Gary That Lulu will love me again?

Simon Well, as you said, she probably does love you, so you better make it that she'll want to shag you again. It's all in the wording.

Pause.

Gary   I don't think so, Si. I mean – it might be my wish, but I don't think it's Lulu's. Then she'd be right, wouldn't she: I really would be a selfish bastard.

Pause.

What about you, Si? What would you wish for – apart from twenty Embassy Filter?

Pause.

Simon   You don't want to know what I'd wish for.

Gary   I do. That's why I asked.

Simon   Probably everything you take for granted. A normal life. With no secrets. A family that could accept me from what I am. A society that could accept me for what I am.

Gary (*pause*)   What are you talking about?

Pause.

Simon   Courage, Simon. It's time to stop living a lie. Speak out with pride. *Carpe Diem.*

Gary *and* **Cherry** *look at each other, then back at* **Simon**.

Simon   Brace yourself for a shock, Gary. I can't live the charade a day longer.

Pause.

I'm gay.

Pause. This has been obvious right from the start.

Cherry   You don't say.

Gary *says nothing.*

Simon   You hate me. I can see it in your eyes. You feel betrayed. But I assure you, Gary, I've never looked at you with a lustful eye. You've been a good friend to me, and if you never wanted to speak to me again I'd understand. But

I can't regret telling you. I feel suddenly lighter, freer than I've ever been. And tomorrow I shall tell my whole family at once. Yes. I'll give them a Queen's speech they'll never fucking forget! (*Pause.*) Gary – will you forgive me?

Gary Er ... yeah, all right, Si.

Cherry Gary – have you noticed that the elf has been very quiet recently?

Pause. As one, they rush to him. They feel for a heartbeat.

Is he dead?!

Gary Difficult to say ...

Simon He's not breathing! Get him onto the floor!

Cherry Untie him!

Simon Oh my God – we've murdered a fucking elf!

Gary Do that thing on his chest!

He makes the palms-down squeezing motion of heart resuscitation.

Simon (*panicked*) How do you do it?!

Gary I don't know, I've only ever seen it on *Baywatch*!

Cherry *gets astride the* **Elf***, and starts doing it. The others running around impotently.*

Gary This isn't going to look very good to the casual observer, is it – ?! He's got rope marks on his wrists and everything!

Gary *rubs the* **Elf***'s wrists.*

Cherry (*to* **Elf**) Come on, come on!

Simon We thought he was an elf, your honour!

Gary That's going to sound great in court!

Cherry Somebody has to give him mouth to mouth!

Pause. **Simon** *and* **Gary** *look at each other. An unsavoury prospect.*

Gary   You're the poofter.

Simon   I like to keep to my own species!

Gary   I thought you didn't believe he was an elf?!

Simon   I've been converted!

Cherry   Somebody – give – him – mouth – to – mouth!!

Gary *attempts it.*

Cherry   Come on, come on, come on –

Simon   You're not supposed to put your tongue in, Gary!
Here –

Simon *takes over the mouth to mouth.*

Cherry   Come on, come on, come on!

Gary   Oh my God!

Simon   Is anything happening?!

Cherry   Nothing!

Simon   I'm doing more blowing than Jeff-fucking-Stryker!

Cherry (*to* **Gary**)   Use your wish!

Gary   Don't be soft!

Cherry   Use your fucking wish!

Gary   I wish the elf would breathe!

Nothing.

Cherry   Again!

Gary   I wish the elf would breathe – I wish the elf would
breathe –

And then **Cherry** *joins in.*

Cherry   I wish the elf would breathe – I wish the elf
would breathe –

And then **Simon** *joins them.*

Simon I wish the elf would breathe – I wish the elf would breathe –

And now they are all saying it:

Gary/Cherry/Simon I wish the elf would breathe! I wish the elf would breathe! I wish the elf would breathe! I wish the elf would breathe! I wish the elf would breathe! I wish the elf would breathe!

*And suddenly, with a huge gulp, the **Elf** starts to breathe, taking in lungfuls of air. The three of them are ecstatic. They lift the **Elf** to his feet. He is bewildered. They are hugging him. They stand back from him. He stares at them wide-eyed.*

Elf What's going on?

Simon We brought you back from the dead!

Cherry We used the wish to bring you back to life!

Gary We've saved Christmas in an exceedingly righteous manner!

Simon Yes, little elf, fly, fly back to Santa! Give our love to Hartlepool!

Cherry Quick, don't ruin it for the children!

Simon Donner and Blitzen, your trusty steeds await!

Gary And Rudolf too, in a state of red-nosedness!

Cherry Quickly!

Pause. He turns and staggers out the door. They wave and shout goodbye. They rush to the window. Pause. They start waving and shouting again. Pause.

Gary There he goes.

Pause. Their laughter and cheering dies off.

Simon That's very lucky to get a taxi so quickly on Christmas Eve.

Cherry Maybe he wished for it.

Pause.

Simon   I wonder where he keeps his change?

Pause. **Gary** *looks at his watch.*

Gary   Here, it's officially Christmas! I've got a bottle!

He rushes off.

Cherry   I wonder if he'll be all right?

Simon   I'm sure he'll get what he needs, one way or another.

Gary *comes in with a bottle of whisky.*

Gary   Here we go!

They all have a swig. Wish each other 'Merry Christmas'. Pause. They calm down.

Cherry   Well, this has been the weirdest Christmas Eve I've spent in a long time.

Pause.

He wasn't an elf, was he?

Gary   Who gives a toss?!

Cherry   Yeah. I mean, everyone thinks kids are so much more open to weird stuff like elves and that. But the older you get, the more you realise there's much weirder stuff than that going on.

Pause.

Simon   Thing is, when you're a kid, all you want is plastic crap. It's when you grow up – that's when you start wanting miracles. That's why we end up with pants and socks. You realise that you're out of Santa's jurisdiction, and well and truly into God's.

Pause.

Cherry   Well. Hate to leave you and all that, but I better get going before Lulu arrives.

Gary Fuck Lulu sideways into a Christmas hamper! We are the three fucking musketeers! I have in my pocket some Christmas feeling powder of the Bolivian marching variety – and between this and the Hungry Hippos, my sweet Cherry, I think I can make it worth your while to take me through the entire Kama Sutra!

Simon Well, it looks like I'll be sitting out of *this* party . . .

Gary Nonsense! You too shall be sucked, fucked and wanked! Ahead of us lies a week of concentrated substance abuse and sensual pleasure. It's swings and roundabouts, mate, swings and roundabouts! Christmas is for children, but complete debauchery is ours!!

They raise their glasses.

All Complete debauchery.

But in their hearts, they know it'll never be quite the same. Music. They pour themselves a refill.

The lights fade.

The Censor

The Censor was commissioned and originally produced by the Red Room. It premiered at the Finborough Theatre, London on 1 April 1997. It was subsequently co-produced with the Royal Court and transferred to the Royal Court Theatre Downstairs at the Duke of York's, London, on 4 June 1997. The cast was as follows:

The Censor	Alastair Galbraith
Miss Fontaine	Racquel Cassidy
The Wife	Alison Newman

Directed by Anthony Neilson
Designed by Julian McGowan
Lighting by Jo Joelson
Sound by Paul Arditti

Characters

The Censor
Miss Fontaine
The Wife

Setting
The play takes place in two locations: the Censor's office and his home.

Censor (*V/O*) It started with a pornographic film. And I swear to God, it was a porn film like any of the hundreds I'd seen.

No: There *were* differences – strange edits and inflections – but at the time I put it down to poor technique.

No: I'll be honest with you – I put it down to the fact it was made by a woman.

The film was hard-core and unpassable as it stood but she requested a meeting with me to challenge the ruling.

I could've refused. To this day, I still don't know if things would've turned out better if I had. But I didn't and she came to try to change my mind, the only way she knew how.

Scene One

The **Censor***'s office.*

Pause.

Censor Miss Fontaine –

Pause.

Please put your shirt back on.

Fontaine Are you married?

Censor No –

Fontaine Are you gay?

Censor *No* – I would just like you to put your *shirt* back on.

Pause.

You're embarrassing me, Miss Fontaine. And you're making a fool of yourself.

Fontaine In what way?

Censor   I don't care to get into a debate about it, all right? Just put your – thing back on . . .

Pause. Her hands go to her bra clip.

Fontaine   Maybe I should take something else off.

Censor   No – !

He stops her. His hands on her arms. Pause. She smiles. He disengages.

Why are you doing this?

Fontaine   Come on, don't act so shocked: you spend all *day* staring at women's breasts –

Censor   I'm not shocked –

Fontaine   Liar. Tell me you haven't dreamt of this: a woman you hardly know offering herself to you? Tell me.

Censor   It's none of your business what I've dreamt of, but whatever I've dreamt of I certainly haven't dreamt of it with you.

Pause.

Fontaine   You will.

Pause.

Censor   Look – please – if somebody comes in –

Pause. She puts her shirt back on.

Fontaine   Suit yourself.

Now she sits down. He is amazed by this.

Censor   I think you'd better go.

Pause. She rises, puts her coat on. Pause.

Fontaine   Will you think about the things I said?

Pause.

About the *film*.

The **Censor** *is at a loss for words.*

Fontaine   I'm not going to be ashamed. Waste of time being ashamed.

Scene Two

The kitchen.

The **Censor's Wife** *wears a dressing-gown. Reads the morning paper.*

Pause.

Censor   What time did you come in?

Wife   Don't know. Four-ish.

Long pause.

Censor   Where did you sleep?

Wife   In the spare room. I didn't want to wake you.

Long pause.

Censor   Where were you?

Wife   Catherine had a few people over for dinner.

Long pause.

Censor   Was David there?

Pause.

Wife   He was there for a while.

Censor *(V/O)*   Fifteen forty-seven: outer labia.

Sixteen o two: inner labia. Penetration by inorganic device.

Sixteen twenty-three: anal penetration by same. Digital insertion to vagina.

Additional oral stimulation of vagina – sixteen forty-two.

Seventeen ten: masturbation of erect penis.

Seventeen twenty-six: oral stimulation of erect penis.

Seventeen fifty-one: repetition of anal insertion sequence.

Eighteen o three: repetition of oral sequence.

Scene Three

The **Censor***'s office.*

He makes her wait as he writes.

Fontaine   You lied to me.

Pause.

You said you weren't married.

Censor   I thought we agreed not to discuss the other night, Miss Fontaine.

Fontaine   I just wondered why you said you weren't married?

Censor   I didn't. I don't know what I said. If I did I didn't mean to. I'm wearing a wedding ring, look. Can we get back to the matter in hand please?

Fontaine   All right.

Pause.

Keep your shirt on.

She smiles. He doesn't. Pause.

So what's the bottom line, Mr Censor?

He makes her wait some more.

Censor   The bottom line is – if you want us to even consider this for release – you'll have to cut somewhere in the region of . . . thirty-five minutes.

Pause.

Fontaine   Which is as good as banning it.

Censor   No, with the cuts I could recommend that it pass as a Restricted 18. It could be sold in licensed video stores.

Fontaine   Sex shops.

Censor   Yes.

Pause.

Look – with all due respect – what did you think was going to happen? Your film is just one sex scene after another. There's no plot, there's no character, there's no nothing. So what did you expect? A tie-in with Burger King?

No: You knew exactly what would happen – that it would cause a fuss, get you some attention. Well it's achieved all that. But whether your film is art, Miss Fontaine, or whether it's pornography, is academic: there are things you just *cannot legally* <u>show</u> here, and that isn't a matter of opinion, it's a matter of *law*.

Pause.

Fontaine   I like how you call me Miss Fontaine.

Censor (*pause*)   Well, I –

Fontaine   No, I like it. Really.

Pause.

You could pass it without classification. It could be shown in cinema clubs.

Censor   Not without cuts.

Fontaine   But with less?

Censor (*sighs*)   Theoretically. But that would require me making a very strong case to the Director.

Fontaine   And are you prepared to do that?

Censor   It'd be a waste of time.

Fontaine   That's not what I asked.

Censor   Miss Fon –

Pause.

Do you have any idea how long it takes to prepare a recommendation? How many forms I'd have to fill out? How many panels it'd have to pass before it reached the top floor? Whole films have been known to just disappear in this system.

Fontaine   I'll take my chances.

Censor   No, but you don't understand – that's films that come from *upstairs*. Coming from down *here* . . .

Fontaine   Down here?

Censor   Has nobody explained this to you? (*Pause.*) D'you know what they call this place, Miss Fontaine? (*Pause.*) 'The *shit hole.*' All we get sent is the sickest, most extreme material. Ninety per cent of what we see is never legally released. Seven per cent of it results in criminal prosecution. About three per cent makes it back into the stream.

The prospects for your film are . . . bleak.

Pause.

Fontaine   So how long have you been . . . 'down here'?

Censor (*pause*)   Six years.

Pause.

But everybody starts here.

Fontaine   Six years is a long start.

Censor   Yes, well I was due for transfer last year but they asked me if I'd . . . stay on a bit longer.

Pause.

Not just anyone can do this job. It requires a strong constitution. It's a compliment really. And it means when I do move on, it'll be to a much better position.

Fontaine   So making a successful recommendation would do you good?

Censor   A *successful* recommendation, yes. But for it to *be* successful, I'd have to believe in the case I was putting. I'd have to believe that your film had some purpose other than titillation.

Fontaine   And you don't.

Pause.

Censor   No. I'm sorry but I don't.

Pause.

It's unusual. I'll admit. Using the same two actors throughout – not always ending in ejaculation, the order of the episodes . . . You might be subverting conventions – but at the end of the day, it's still just hard-core pornography. And I have no *problem* with that! In fact I'm quite *liberal* in my attitude towards it. But let's call a spade a spade, shall we? Let's not pretend it's groundbreaking art, as if I'm so green I won't know the difference. *That* is just a wee bit too *insulting*.

Fontaine   So why'd you call me back in? If you're just a 'wee bit too insulted'?

Pause.

Censor   Because I know what you think: that I'm a prude, a stuffed shirt – some sort of repressed, anally retentive apparatchik –

Fontaine   You *like* to tell people what they think, don't you?

Censor (*weary*)   No, because I know you walked out of here the other night thinking you'd oh-so-cleverly shown me up for what I am –

Fontaine   I wondered when we'd get back to that.

Censor   Well yes because it's outrageous behaviour – I mean, what am I supposed to do, this woman I've never met before just starts taking her *clothes* off – I mean *anyone* would be a bit . . . *taken aback* by that, but to you it just confirms this smug, simplistic notion that anyone who does this job must be some . . . sort of . . .

Fontaine   Repressed anally retentive apparatchik?

Censor   Yes, that's right –

Fontaine   You think that's why I did it?

Censor   I don't *know* why you did it! I've no *idea* – !

Fontaine   Maybe I just wanted to.

Censor   Wanted to humiliate me maybe –

Fontaine   Wanted to understand you.

Censor   No, because I don't appreciate being made to feel like a fool, Miss Fontaine! You can't just walk in here and make a fool out of me, d'you understand?!

Pause.

She advances on him.

Fontaine   So that's why you called me back? To tell me I couldn't make a fool of you?

Censor   Yes – well, no – to tell you the – the reasons for – my decision –

Fontaine   I don't believe you.

Censor   Miss Fontaine –

Fontaine   You thought of me, didn't you?

Censor   No I didn't – well yes obviously I did – but not in the way –

Fontaine   The little seeds turned into a beanstalk like I knew they would.

She puts her hand on his crotch.

Censor   Please don't do that –

Fontaine   Stop me.

He makes a weak attempt to remove her hand. She starts to unzip his fly.

What's protecting you, Mr Censor? That's what I want to know.

She begins to masturbate him. This goes on for some time, to no avail.

You're not relaxed then.

Pause. She removes her hand. He does his flies up. She smells her hand.

Talcum powder. I'm impressed. A hint of urine but that can't be helped. Do you normally smell so sweet, or are you expecting a road accident?

Pause.

Censor   Why are you doing this? Really?

Pause.

It won't make any difference to my decision, if that's what you're thinking.

Pause.

Do you have some sort of mental problem? No, I'm being serious: are you on medication of some kind?

Fontaine   You've got a very low opinion of yourself.

Censor   This is nothing to do with *me*!

Fontaine   Isn't it?

Censor   You don't *know* me!

Fontaine   I know you a lot better than if I'd kept my shirt on.

Pause.

Censor   This isn't right.

Fontaine Because you're married?

Censor That's one reason.

Fontaine What would your wife say if I called her up and told her I'd just had my hand down her husband's trousers?

Pause.

Censor Are you threatening me, Miss Fontaine?

Fontaine No, it's hypothetical. What would she say?

Pause.

Censor My wife and I have a very specific policy regarding infidelities in our marriage.

Fontaine And what's that?

Pause.

Censor She tells me about them.

Pause.

Fontaine Oh. I see.

Pause.

That must be . . . humiliating.

Censor (*pause*) Not for me.

Pause.

Fontaine Haven't you ever had an affair?

Pause.

Censor Why am I even *thinking* about answering that? That's none of your business, is it?

Pause. She looks puzzled.

Fontaine But we're having one, aren't we?

Censor (*pause*) One what?

Fontaine An affair.

Censor An *affair*??!!

Fontaine Well . . . after what we did . . .

Censor After what *we* did?! You stuck your hand down my *trousers*!!

Fontaine Are we going to squabble over the details or are we going to try and work this out like adults?

Censor (*flabbergasted*) Miss Fontaine – we are *not* having an affair – !

Fontaine But I've touched your genitals!

Censor I didn't *ask* you to touch them, did I?!

Fontaine Did though!

Censor There's more to it than that, surely to God!!

Fontaine I don't believe so.

Censor So I become an adulterer the minute you put your hand down my trousers?!

Fontaine No – the minute you put talc down your *boxers*.

Pause. She can't keep the joke up any longer.

I *know* we're not having an affair. So stop acting like we are.

Pause.

Censor Miss Fontaine – I can honestly say – that you are one of the most *bizarre* people I've ever met –

Pause.

Fontaine This film is important. Do you understand how important it is?

Censor (*pause*) I can see it means a lot to you.

Fontaine No. Not just to me. To the world.

Pause.

Censor That I don't see. I'm sorry, but I don't.

Pause.

Fontaine   You will.

Scene Four

The kitchen.

Wife   He wants to talk to you.

Pause.

Censor   What about?

Wife   You know . . .

Pause.

The situation.

Pause.

I said I didn't know.

Scene Five

Censor   All right. Let's start with the last section.

Fontaine   Why the last section?

Censor   Because it's the most problematic.

Fontaine   But it's the end of the story.

Pause.

Censor   And what story is this, Miss Fontaine?

Fontaine   The story of the lovers.

Censor   Lovers, is that what they are?

Fontaine   What else would they be?

Pause.

Censor (*sighs*)   All right.

Pause.

Scene one. (*Reads.*) Man is masturbated by woman.

Pause.

That is scene one, isn't it? It's not a prologue? Man is masturbated by woman.

Fontaine   Is that all you saw?

Censor   There wasn't much else to see.

Fontaine   Because your eye stops at the image.

Censor   Most people's would.

Fontaine   Because they've lost the ability to see.

Censor   And what is there to see in a penis exactly?! A penis is a penis, is it not?

Fontaine   What about when it's your wife's lover's penis?

Pause.

Censor   You're overstepping the mark, Miss Fontaine.

Fontaine   *You* told me about it.

Censor   I shouldn't have. I don't know why I did.

Fontaine   Because I touched your genitals.

Censor   *Please*!!

Pause.

Now you asked me to help you! I don't have to after the way you've behaved but I'm giving you this chance to prove your point. So I don't want to hear any more about that incident. It should never have happened and that's that. Now can we discuss the man being masturbated by the woman, please? What exactly is the 'story' of that?

Fontaine   Well, the man's penis hardens and softens repeatedly throughout the scene.

Pause.

Censor   It's not exactly *The Maltese Falcon*, is it?

Fontaine   But *why* did it do that?

Censor   Why did it tumesce and detumesce repeatedly?
(*Pause.*) I don't know, Miss Fontaine. Was the actor
camera-shy?

Fontaine   You're confusing the actor with the man, Mr
Censor. Why did it happen to the man?

Pause.

Why would he not be able to stay erect whilst she
masturbated him?

Pause.

Censor   Maybe she wasn't very good at it.

Fontaine   Maybe. But why not?

Censor   I don't know, is she a nun?

Pause.

Fontaine   Put your fingers in me.

Pause.

Censor   What?

Fontaine   Put your fingers inside me.

Pause.

Censor   Why?

Fontaine   Just trust me.

Pause.

Censor   I won't be able to hold my pen.

Pause. She guides him in.

Miss Fontaine – please – we can't do this –

Fontaine   Just hold it there. That's nice.

Pause.

All right: her strokes were erratic, random. She didn't know his rhythm. So that means . . . ?

Pause.

So that *means* – ?

Censor Uh – that means – they haven't . . . done it . . . before?

Fontaine (*nods*) This is the early part of the relationship. They're still learning about each other.
Deeper.

He pushes his fingers deeper. She winces, laughing at his mistake.

Deeper into the *story* . . .

Censor Sorry – the story – sorry . . .

Fontaine Did you notice that the man's penis only stiffened when he could see her stroking it?

Pause. He shakes his head.

He's visual rather than tactile.

Censor So why didn't . . . why didn't he just keep . . . looking at her?

Fontaine Probably he watches a lot of pornography and he thinks she might see that in his eyes and feel like a whore.

Pause.

You could move those fingers about a bit if you like.

He does.

He likes her. He thinks they might have a future.

Pause.

And that's why.

Censor Why . . . ?

Fontaine Because he needs distance. Engagement scares him.

Pause.

Censor   What else?

Fontaine   You want me to tell you?

He nods.

Are you sure?

He nods.

He's wary of people, solitary.
Parents were cerebral rather than physical and he's the same.
When he lived at home, his bedroom was next door to theirs.
One parent was very ill –

He withdraws his fingers. Pause.

Censor   Are you playing some sort of trick on me, Miss Fontaine?

Pause.

Has someone put you up to this?

Pause.

You were describing the character in your film?

Fontaine   Why? Does he sound familiar?

Pause.

Censor   And you're expecting people to get all that, are you? Just from watching that scene?
That his bedroom was next door to theirs?

Fontaine   A penis is not just a penis.

Censor   Well you might as well say a hatstand's not a bloody . . . *hatstand*!

Fontaine   The difference is we're allowed to see hatstands.

Pause.

Censor I don't know why you're wasting your time with this.
You're obviously – an intelligent woman.
You don't need to show genitalia to get your point across.

Fontaine That's true. But what *you're* saying is you don't think I *should*.

Censor *I'm* not saying anything – !

Fontaine Coward.

Censor I'm just saying that . . . censorship isn't necessarily such . . . a bad thing. Without censorship, there'd be no allegory, no metaphor, no restraint –
I mean – *Brief Encounter* is a story about two lovers, but you don't have to see Trevor Howard's penis thrusting in and out of Celia Johnson, do you?

Pause. She smiles.

But you'd like that wouldn't you? You'd *like* to see Trevor Howard's penis thrusting in and out of Celia Johnson!
That's exactly what you'd like!

But her smile infects him and he finds himself laughing.

A moment.

Scene Six

Wife What's funny?

Pause.

He doesn't want to be your enemy.
He's got nothing against you.

Pause.

He just wants you to see there are feelings involved here.

Pause.

Censor   What do *you* want?

Pause.

Wife   Yes. I want that too.

Scene Seven

The **Censor** *waits and waits. He places a bottle of wine and two glasses on the desk, considers them for a while and then decides against it. Eventually she arrives.*

Censor   You're almost an hour late, Miss Fontaine.

Fontaine   I know, I couldn't help it.

Pause.

Censor   If you want to make this preliminary recommendation deadline then you'll need all the time I can spare and that's not much. And now it's an hour less.

Pause.

Fontaine   I brought you some flowers.

She hands them to him. He stares at them. Pause.

Censor   Thank you.

Pause. They look around. Nowhere to put them. Delicately, he lays them down on the desk.

Actually, I have something too.

He produces a bottle of wine and some glasses.

Seeing as it's after hours . . .

He starts to pour it.

Fontaine   Not for me, thanks.

Censor (*pause*)   No?

No. He pours himself one.

She reads his notes.

Fontaine MILKY MAMAS – what's that?

Censor It's pregnant women having sex with each other.

Fontaine (*genuinely*) That's nice . . .

Pause.

Censor Yes, well – pornography's nothing if not diverse. Cheers.

Pause.

You know it's a funny thing, Miss Fontaine, but I can't imagine you travelling here. I can't imagine you sitting on a bus or going shopping. Doing anything normal.

I suppose you've got friends you go out with, that sort of thing?

Fontaine *shrugs.*

Fontaine You're not the only person that finds me bizarre.

Censor Well, I wouldn't say *bizarre* exactly: you just take a bit of getting used to.

Fontaine And are you? Used to me?

Censor I'm . . . getting there.

Pause.

Fontaine So when are you going to hang up your scissors, Mr Censor? When people just give up having sex altogether?
Will that be the job done?

Censor No, no, not at all. We'll move on to humour next. Eventually we'll have eradicated all pleasure from the world. It's called Scottish expansionism.

She shows no sign of amusement.

No, nobody's trying to eradicate sex, Miss Fontaine.
There's just a few of us who still believe it should be about love. I know that's terribly old-fashioned . . .

Fontaine It's not old-fashioned.

Censor (*pause*) No, well I'm –

Fontaine It's just completely stupid. Love is an emotion, sex is a means of expression. You can't restrict a language to one emotion.

Pause.

Censor So in that case the – the things we've – *done*: what do they – express – exactly?

Pause.

Fontaine Trust.

Censor Trust. (*Pause.*) Good. (*Pause.*) Good.

Fontaine Curiosity . . .

Censor (*nods*) Uh-huh . . . ?

Fontaine Many things.

He nods. Pause.

Scene two?

Censor Yes. Right. Scene two.

Consults clipboard.

Intercourse.

Fontaine Is that it?

Censor (*sighs*) Eight o six: erect penis –
Eight eighteen: inner labia –
Eight thirty-one: vaginal penetration.

Fontaine Position?

Censor (*pause*) Missionary.

Fontaine That's right: not from behind, not standing up – the most *traditional* position. And so?

Censor (*sighs*) All right – scene one, they're getting to know each other. So now – they know each other better?

Pause.

Look – we don't have time for this.
Why don't you just *tell* me?

Fontaine   Because I want you to *see*! You time code
every single detail of genital interplay, but you don't see
the *looks* that pass between them, the *breathing*, the *rhythms* – !

Censor   Because those are not my *concerns*, Miss Fontaine!
The looks, the breathing, the rhythms aren't the reason
your film can't be passed!! You have to be *practical* about
this! It doesn't matter *how* sincere you are, we can't change
the *law*!

Pause. She takes her knickers off, lies on the floor.

Fontaine   Come on.

Censor   Miss Fontaine –

Fontaine   I want you to have sex with me.

Pause.

Censor   It's not going to make any difference.

Fontaine   We'll see.

Pause.

Censor   I can't.

Fontaine   Why not?

Censor   Because it's not *right*.

Fontaine   It's not right, it's not right. Your *job* isn't *right*,
Mr Censor! Your *marriage* isn't *right*! And if we're talking
about ethics, then buying that bottle of wine probably
wasn't *right*, was it? For someone who's always talking about
what's *right*, you seem to have an awful lot *wrong*!

Censor   Oh, and you have such *insight*, don't you?! Well
it's *you* that's got it wrong this time, Miss Fontaine, because
I'm not *talking* about ethics!

Pause.

That's *not* what I'm talking about.

Fontaine   What, then?

Pause.

Censor   You were wrong about the talcum powder.

Pause.

I have to use a . . .

Pause.

I have to use a special shampoo.

Pause.

I had a bit of a . . . *problem* . . .

Fontaine (*pause*)   An infection?

Censor   Not exactly.

Pause.

I think they call it . . . an infestation.

Fontaine   Did you get them from your wife?

Pause.

Censor   You don't just get them from sex. You can get them from toilet seats.

Pause.

Fontaine   And that's why you can't have sex with me?

Pause. She stands up.

Liar.

Censor (*pause*)   You can think what you like.

Fontaine   So you let me touch your genitals knowing you had an 'infestation'?

Censor   I don't remember having much choice.

Fontaine   Liar. You've never scratched yourself *once.*

Pause.

Censor   I said I *had* them –

Fontaine   Ah – hah!

Censor   But you have to complete the treatment before it's completely safe! That's *true*.

Fontaine   Well, I've never had an infestation before. It might be interesting.

Censor   Oh grow up, for God's sake!

Fontaine   Why don't you want to have sex with me?

Censor   Does there *have* to be a reason?!

Fontaine   No, but there *is* one. And it's strong enough to use your 'infestation' as a cover.

Pause.

Censor   Has it ever occurred to you, Miss Fontaine, that maybe I'm just not attracted to you? Has that ever crossed your mind?!

Fontaine   No.

Pause.

Censor   Well that's just . . . very . . . arrogant of you . . .

Fontaine   Tell me the *truth*.

Censor   I just don't *feel* like doing it, all right?

Fontaine   You don't have to *feel* like doing it. You just have to do it.

Censor   I don't *want* to do it!

Fontaine   You mean you couldn't do it.

Pause.

Censor   Well yes, I could physically *do* it. I could just . . . *do* it.

Fontaine   Come on then.

She lies down. Pause.

Censor   Is that what you want, for me to just . . . ?

Fontaine   Do it. Yes.

Pause.

Censor (*shrugs*)   All right. If that's really what you want.

Reluctantly, he sets about undoing trousers and so on.

But I'm telling you – you're taking a risk –

She nods. But he cannot go through with it. Pause.

Fontaine   What's wrong?

Censor   Nothing it's just – not really a very conducive atmosphere, is it?

Fontaine   You don't have to perform. I just want to show you something.

Censor   That's what I *mean*: it's all a bit clinical . . .

Fontaine   D'you want me to help you?

Censor   No, I'm fine.

Fontaine   Look at my vagina if that helps.

Pause.

Censor   Miss Fontaine – I'm just not that sort of . . .

It's not that easy for me to just . . . you know.

I'm not one of those men that can just do it at the drop of a hat. Never have been.

Fontaine   You're always connecting penises with hats, are you aware of that?

Pause.

Do you have a problem with impotence?

Censor   *No.*

Fontaine   You can tell me.

Censor   I *don't*.

Pause.

I'm just . . . not that easily . . . you know . . . *stimulated*.

Fontaine   Are you worried about the size of your penis?

Censor   No, not really. I'm fairly realistic about all that.

Long pause.

Why, should I be?

Fontaine (*shrugs*)   No.

Pause.

Are you like this with your wife?

Censor   Well . . . we don't really . . . do it that much.

Fontaine   Have her infidelities affected your libido?

Pause.

Censor   Well, obviously it's not what you'd call a *boost* to the ego but . . .

Pause.

It's probably more the other way round.

Fontaine   Explain?

Pause.

Censor   It's like I said: I've never been that . . . physical a person.

Pause.

I know men are supposed to be obsessed with it, and ready to do it whenever, wherever, with *who*ever. But I think that's a bit of a myth.

Pause.

I don't want you to think my wife's some kind of . . . (*Pause.*) It's not like that.

She doesn't *deceive* me.
I always have the choice to leave. So far I've chosen to stay.

Pause.

Things just happen, don't they? You meet people. And she's a very physical person. Not just sex: she likes to dance and just . . . go mad now and then. That's just *her*.

Someone comes along and they're new and exciting and . . . well, you know . . .

Pause.

What we have isn't based on sex.

Long pause.

Fontaine You're impotent, aren't you.

Pause.

Censor You know, Miss Fontaine, you are about the most arrogant person I've ever met. What's this latest theory based on? Because I won't just get on the floor and have sex with you?

Pause.

And even if I was – which I'm not – what difference would it make?

Pause.

Fontaine There's no point in any of this if I can't make you see.

Pause.

Censor But I *do* see! I know I'm making out that I don't – but I just want to give you the – you know – the other angle. I mean it's an interesting idea but you know – it's not exactly beyond my grasp. And you have a point. You do.

I think we should try to get it through.

She looks at him, dubious.

Really. I think I can even draft something up for the next session.

I just need to watch it again. Just let me do that.

Scene Eight

Wife   So?

Pause.

Will you *meet* him?

Long pause.

Say something!

Lights fade to black.

Scene Nine

The **Censor** *is pleased with himself.*

Censor   All right, listen to this. Are you listening?

She nods.

(*Reads.*) 'Miss Fontaine's intention is to depict the course of a relationship, from courtship to separation, by focusing exclusively on the couple's sexual activity.

'Thus, masturbation and oral sex denote courtship, and intercourse in the missionary position symbolises a *traditional* vow of commencement. During this stage of infatuation, with the future uncertain, the sexual activities are essentially conservative.

'But as trust deepens, and a sense of ownership develops, the activities become more various and individualised, the bodies more objectified.' – Yes?

She remains impassive.

All right, I don't know about this, listen to this:
'An aggressive note is introduced as the couple pass
through their first <u>betrayal</u>. –

'This disillusionment opens a phase of experimentation now
more animalistic, more overtly passionate and more
stereotypically divided along crude gender lines.

'*But* – whilst this new element of distrust invigorates the
sexuality, the spiritual basis of the relationship erodes until
copulation becomes their only cement.

'As a result, we enter the realms of depersonalisation: the
sexuality intensifies, becoming more abusive, more
fetishistic, a rehearsal for separation. And even after this
separation, they still participate in sporadic erotic
encounters until new partners are found.

'*Finally*' – and this bit took me ages to get – 'we see each
partner participate in solitary acts of masturbation, their
memories of each other now just the fuel of their fantasies.'
– Now *that* sounds like art, doesn't it?

She looks unimpressed.

So? Do I pass with honours?

Pause.

Fontaine   Is that *all* you saw?

Pause.

Censor   That's a joke, isn't it?

Fontaine (*pause*)   I told you all this the first day we *met*!
All you've done is state the obvious, albeit in that rather
mechanistic way of yours.

Censor   The *obvious*?! –

Fontaine   Where's the character, the subtext, the
detail – ?

Censor   The character, the – ?!! Are you being *serious*?!

It's <u>two</u> people, on a <u>bed</u> – <u>wanking</u> and <u>shagging</u> and

sucking each other off!! That's all it is! There isn't even
any *dialogue*!!

Pause.

Fontaine You don't see it.

Censor But I *do*! I *see* the relationship! I see what you're
trying to do!
I doubt if anyone *else* will! But that's *it*!
There's nothing else to be had from it! And if you think
there *is*, then ... − !

Fontaine Then what?

Pause.

Censor Then I don't know if I can help you any more.

Pause.

Fontaine You have to.

Censor Why do I have to?

Fontaine I told you: this film is important ...

Censor To the world. Yes, I remember.

Fontaine I'm serious!
You think the world will stay this way?
You think this is the highest level we'll reach?
Read the newspapers, Mr Censor: artificial insemination,
cloning, male contraception −
Very soon, sex will be completely divorced from
reproduction.
You think it'll just disappear?
No, It'll be free to evolve into the most sophisticated level
of interaction attainable: a completely universal non-verbal
language.

Think about that! What that'll *mean*!
No more repression! No more witch-hunts − A world
absolutely without guilt or shame! And one by one all the
institutions that've got fat on that shame − the church, the

courts, the social services, even this rotten building we're in now – they'll fall, Mr Censor! They'll come crashing down!

And the people we dare to call perverts and deviants – the victims of this war – the good humane people we've criminalised and traumatised, they'll be recognised for what they truly are: Visionaries! (*Pause.*) Visionaries.

And that's why you have to learn to *see*! Because you go on about *Brief Encounter* but this subtlety you cherish so much, it's just lies, that's all, lies dressed up as good taste and yes this film is every *bit* as rich, every *bit* as moving, every *bit* as detailed.
This film is the first artefact of a truly liberated future. And the day it can be shown in every multiplex in the land to every man, woman and child is the day we'll know the human race has come of age.

Now, it's good that you see the relationship, but that's only the first level. Could you tell, for instance, that the man's previous girlfriend was Asian? That the woman had been brought up in care? Could you see any of that?

Long pause.

Censor   No. (*Pause.*) I couldn't.

Fontaine   It's there, right in front of your eyes. If you can see beyond the image.

Pause.

Censor   Why me, Miss Fontaine? Why's it so important that *I* should see all this? Because you think I can help you?

Fontaine   You can.

Censor   I told you what they call this place.
We're virtually lepers down here.
I go to the canteen, people move to another table.
I don't even have access past the third floor.

Pause.

D'you understand? I can't guarantee this recommendation will pass. I just don't have the power. So if it's *that* – if it's just *that* – then you're wasting your time with me.

Pause.

Is it just that?

Pause.

Fontaine   I want you to see.

She kneels down in front of him, puts her hand on his crotch.

I was right, wasn't I? You are impotent.

Pause.

Censor   You're just guessing. You don't know.

Pause.

Fontaine   I was right about one of your parents being ill, wasn't I?

Censor   Someone told you. You found out somehow. It doesn't prove anything.

Fontaine   There were many infidelities because of that illness. You saw how sex can destroy lives. But they loved each other too, and that was the most confusing thing. Because for all your talk about sex meaning love, it's *you* that can't bring them together. If you could, you wouldn't still be with your wife. No, sex is as much a mystery to you as happiness is. Something you can only watch and envy. But all that's obvious. There's something more specific. Your impotence isn't medical. This is about shame.

You have a fantasy you're ashamed of.

You think of your wife as this deeply sexual being but you know even she wouldn't approve of it. Maybe you even asked her to do it once.

Yes and she was digusted, wasn't she? And if this highly sexual woman could be so disgusted, who else would ever be different?

But you know there are girls that do it. You've seen it on the screen. Girls being forced to degrade themselves to feed the sordid fantasies of misfits like you. And you hate those misfits, don't you? You hate them because they're too weak to rise above their desires. And where are we if we can't rise above our desires? You've done it. But you've paid a price, haven't you?

So what could this fantasy be?

Censor   Miss Fontaine – this is all very – entertaining but –

Fontaine   If it was sado-masochistic you could easily indulge it with prostitutes, and anyway you're visual not tactile. This is about watching. Watching something taboo. Somewhere in your childhood, you saw this thing and had your first strong sexual feeling. You haven't buried it. You know what it is because you think about it when you masturbate.

Pause.

What did you see? Was it inside?

Pause. Her hand on his crotch.

No. Outside then? (*Pause.*) Something taboo. Something violent? (*Pause.*) No.

Pause. She smiles.

Oh, Mr Censor. How beautiful. How absolutely beautiful.

Scene Ten

Miss Fontaine *lays newspaper down on the floor.*

The **Censor** *watches.*

Fontaine *encourages him to touch himself.*

She raises her skirt and squats. The **Censor** *watches, touching himself more vigorously.*

It takes her a while, but eventually she defecates.

She cleans herself, then moves away.

The **Censor** *is in a state of extreme arousal.*

She beckons him to come forward and make love to her.

He does.

Scene Eleven

Wife   All right. Have it your way.

We'll just pretend nothing's happening, shall we?
I'll read my paper and you sit there staring into space and
we'll just hope it goes away like we've always done.

Pause.

Scene Twelve

Long pause.

Censor   Where are you going?

Fontaine   New York.

Pause.

Censor   Another film?

Fontaine   No. (*Pause.*) An installation. At a gallery.

Pause.

Censor   When?

Fontaine   Tomorrow morning. Seven o'clock.

Pause. The **Censor** *exhales, winded by the news. Pause.*

It's all happened very quickly.

Censor   Yes . . .

Pause.

Well, you know – we can continue when you get back –

Fontaine   Yes. All right.

Pause. She stands, preparing to go.

Censor   So does this installation involve getting repressed, anally retentive apparatchiks to look beyond the image?

Fontaine (*faint smile*)   No. They're all very avant-garde. Believe it or not, there's a few people even *I* find bizarre.

Censor   Well – thank God for that.

Long pause.

Have I done something?

Fontaine   Like what?

Censor   I don't know.

Pause.

Like you said: it's all happened very quickly.

Pause. She extends her hand.

Fontaine   Thank you for your help, Mr Censor. I appreciate it.

Pause.

Censor   Why are you being like this?

Fontaine   Like what?

Censor (*pause*)   Well what about the film?

Pause.

My time's valuable, you know. I can't afford to go wasting it on whimsical little projects that you can just walk away from when it suits you.

Pause.

Fontaine   It doesn't suit me.

Pause. He puts her hand on his crotch.

Gently, she removes it. He places it back again.

Censor   Please. Don't be like this.

He uses her hand to touch himself.

You know all these things about me, but I don't know anything about you.

Pause.

There's time for that, isn't there?

Fontaine   Yes. I'm sure there is.

She removes her hand.

But not just now.

Pause.

Censor   You're not the only person who sees things, you know. I see a few things too.

Fontaine (*pause*)   What do you see?

Censor   Things maybe you don't.

Pause.

Fontaine   What?

Censor   I see someone who's running away from herself. Someone who's running away from the truth.

Fontaine   The truth.

Pause.

Censor   Something happened to you.

Fontaine   What?

Censor   I don't know. Something.

Fontaine   Oh I see. You need an explanation.

Pause.

Censor   You like to think you're on some higher level but you're just as fucked as everyone else. All that stuff about artefacts and visionaries, I mean *listen* to yourself – !

Fontaine   I have to go now.

He intercepts her, physically stopping her.

Censor   Don't. Not yet.

Pause.

I've just – I've been looking forward to – talking to you –

Fontaine   I know, but I've got things to do –

Censor   They can wait ten minutes, can't they?!

Fontaine   Let go of me.

Pause.

Censor   Is this because of . . . what we did?

Fontaine   No.

Censor   Because I wouldn't ask you to do it again –

Fontaine   You didn't ask the first time.

Censor   No, that's right I didn't. I didn't ask for *any* of this –

Fontaine (*pause*)   Let go of my wrists.

Censor   Don't talk to me like that, as if I'm just some *stranger*!

Fontaine   I'm not. I just have to go.

Censor   All of a sudden you just have to go? And that's nothing to do with the other night?

Fontaine   No. Nothing.

Censor   Liar. I can see the disgust in your eyes.

Fontaine   No –

Censor   No, it's all right. You dug down into me and

now you're disgusted by what you found. But it's you that did it. I didn't ask you to. It's you that squatted there with everything showing and did it, so maybe you should save some of that disgust for yourself – !

He has shaken her too violently. He lets go of her, shocked by his lack of control.

Pause.

I'm sorry. I didn't mean that. Really.

It's just – I've never – I've never felt –

He embraces her. She does not resist. Her hands run up his back. They breathe together.

They kiss.

Eventually they separate.

You'll call me when you get back, won't you?

Pause. She nods.

I'm going to sort it all out with my wife.

Pause.

I'm just saying.

Fontaine Good.

She walks away.

Censor I'll do some more work on the recommendation.

She climbs the staircase.

But there's only so much I can do. I still can't see what you see.

She stops at the top of the staircase.

Fontaine Don't worry.

Pause.

You will.

Scene Thirteen

Wife *sits, wearing dressing-gown and reading the morning paper.*

Censor   What time did you come in?

Wife   Don't know. Four-ish.

Long pause.

Censor   Where did you sleep?

Wife   In the spare room. I didn't want to wake you.

Pause.

Censor   Where were you?

Wife   Catherine had a few people over for dinner.

Long pause.

Censor   Was David there?

Wife (*pause*)   He was there for a while.

Long pause.

He wants to talk to you.

Pause.

Censor   What about?

Wife   You know . . .

Pause.

The situation.

Pause.

I said I didn't know.

Pause. He smiles.

What's funny?

Pause.

He doesn't want to be your enemy.

He's got nothing against you.

Pause.

He just wants you to see there are feelings involved here.

Pause.

Censor   What do *you* want?

Pause.

Wife   Yes. I want that too.

Pause.

So?

Pause.

(*Exasperated.*) Will you *meet* him?

Long pause.

Say something!

Pause.

All right. Have it your way.
We'll just pretend nothing's happening, shall we?
I'll read my paper and you sit there staring into space and
we'll just hope it goes away like we've always done.

Pause.

Censor   No, I'll say something.

Wife   No, fuck it, Frank.
Go and have your egg and your . . . toast fucking soldiers.

Long pause.

Censor   There's no point in meeting him.

Wife   If you say so.

Pause.

Censor   There's no point in meeting him because –

Wife   Don't you know this woman?

Censor Listen to me –

Wife Shirley Fontaine – Didn't she make that film you were working on?

Pause.

Censor She's in the paper?

Wife She's been murdered – (*Pause.*) Yes, look – She was working on an exhibition – 'controversial film which was recently banned by the Board of Classification' – *must* be the same person –

Long pause.

Censor What uh ...

Pause.

What ... happened?

Pause.

Wife She was beaten to death in a hotel room. In New York. (*Pause.*) God, what a horrible way to go.

Pause.

Did you actually meet her?

Pause.

Censor Um ... no ... not really ... I ... um ...

He tries to control himself, but the tears come.

Pause. She sees he is upset.

Wife Look – I'm sorry. I know this is hard for you, but it's hard for all of us. And you just don't say anything.

He is breaking down, shuddering, making those strange noises that grief causes.

She goes to him, comforts him.

You don't have to meet him. I just don't know what else to do.

Pause.

We'll work it out. We always do.

Scene Fourteen

The **Censor** *sits in his office, watching the film.*
And, after a while, he smiles.

A SELECTED LIST OF
METHUEN MODERN PLAYS

☐ CLOSER	Patrick Marber	£6.99
☐ THE BEAUTY QUEEN OF LEENANE	Martin McDonagh	£6.99
☐ A SKULL IN CONNEMARA	Martin McDonagh	£6.99
☐ THE LONESOME WEST	Martin McDonagh	£6.99
☐ THE CRIPPLE OF INISHMAAN	Martin McDonagh	£6.99
☐ THE STEWARD OF CHRISTENDOM	Sebastian Barry	£6.99
☐ SHOPPING AND F***ING	Mark Ravenhill	£6.99
☐ FAUST (FAUST IS DEAD)	Mark Ravenhill	£5.99
☐ POLYGRAPH	Robert Lepage and Marie Brassard	£6.99
☐ BEAUTIFUL THING	Jonathan Harvey	£6.99
☐ MEMORY OF WATER & FIVE KINDS OF SILENCE	Shelagh Stephenson	£7.99
☐ WISHBONES	Lucinda Coxon	£6.99
☐ BONDAGERS & THE STRAW CHAIR	Sue Glover	£9.99
☐ SOME VOICES & PALE HORSE	Joe Penhall	£7.99
☐ KNIVES IN HENS	David Harrower	£6.99
☐ BOYS' LIFE & SEARCH AND DESTROY	Howard Korder	£8.99
☐ THE LIGHTS	Howard Korder	£6.99
☐ SERVING IT UP & A WEEK WITH TONY	David Eldridge	£8.99
☐ INSIDE TRADING	Malcolm Bradbury	£6.99
☐ MASTERCLASS	Terrence McNally	£5.99
☐ EUROPE & THE ARCHITECT	David Grieg	£7.99
☐ BLUE MURDER	Peter Nichols	£6.99
☐ BLASTED & PHAEDRA'S LOVE	Sarah Kane	£7.99

• All Methuen Drama books are available through mail order or from your local bookshop.

Please send cheque/eurocheque/postal order (sterling only) Access, Visa, Mastercard, Diners Card, Switch or Amex.

☐☐☐☐☐☐☐☐☐☐☐☐☐☐☐☐

Expiry Date: _____ Signature: _____

Please allow 75 pence per book for post and packing U.K.
Overseas customers please allow £1.00 per copy for post and packing.

ALL ORDERS TO:

Methuen Books, Books by Post, TBS Limited, The Book Service, Colchester Road, Frating Green, Colchester, Essex CO7 7DW.

NAME: _____

ADDRESS: _____

_____

_____

Please allow 28 days for delivery. Please tick box if you do not
wish to receive any additional information ☐

Prices and availability subject to change without notice.

METHUEN CLASSICAL GREEK DRAMATISTS

☐ AESCHYLUS PLAYS: I (*Persians, Prometheus Bound, Suppliants, Seven Against Thebes*) £9.99
☐ AESCHYLUS PLAYS: II (*Oresteia: Agamemnon, Libation-Bearers, Eumenides*) £9.99
☐ SOPHOCLES PLAYS: I (*Oedipus the King, Oedipus at Colonus, Antigone*) £9.99
☐ SOPHOCLES PLAYS: II (*Ajax, Women of Trachis, Electra, Philoctetes*) £9.99
☐ EURIPIDES PLAYS: I (*Medea, The Phoenician Women, Bacchae*) £9.99
☐ EURIPIDES PLAYS: II (*Hecuba, The Women of Troy, Iphigenia at Aulis, Cyclops*) £9.99
☐ EURIPIDES PLAYS: III (*Alkestis, Helen, Ion*) £9.99
☐ EURIPIDES PLAYS: IV (*Elektra, Orestes, Iphigeneia in Tauris*) £9.99
☐ EURIPIDES PLAYS: V (*Andromache, Herakles' Children, Herakles*) £9.99
☐ EURIPIDES PLAYS: VI (*Hippolytos Suppliants, Rhesos*) £9.99
☐ ARISTOPHANES PLAYS: I (*Acharnians, Knights, Peace, Lysistrata*) £9.99
☐ ARISTOPHANES PLAYS: II (*Wasps, Clouds, Birds, Festival Time, Frogs*) £9.99
☐ ARISTOPHANES & MENANDER: NEW COMEDY
(Aristophanes: *Women in Power, Wealth*
Menander: *The Malcontent, The Woman from Samos*) £9.99

• All Methuen Drama books are available through mail order or from your local bookshop.

Please send cheque/eurocheque/postal order (sterling only) Access, Visa, Mastercard, Diners Card, Switch or Amex.

☐☐☐☐☐☐☐☐☐☐☐☐☐☐☐☐

Expiry Date: _____ Signature: _____

Please allow 75 pence per book for post and packing U.K.
Overseas customers please allow £1.00 per copy for post and packing.

ALL ORDERS TO:

Methuen Books, Books by Post, TBS Limited, The Book Service, Colchester Road, Frating Green, Colchester, Essex CO7 7DW.

NAME: _____

ADDRESS: _____

_____

_____

Please allow 28 days for delivery. Please tick box if you do not
wish to receive any additional information ☐

Prices and availability subject to change without notice.

METHUEN STUDENT EDITIONS

☐ SERJEANT MUSGRAVE'S DANCE	John Arden	£6.99
☐ CONFUSIONS	Alan Ayckbourn	£5.99
☐ THE ROVER	Aphra Behn	£5.99
☐ LEAR	Edward Bond	£6.99
☐ THE CAUCASIAN CHALK CIRCLE	Bertolt Brecht	£6.99
☐ MOTHER COURAGE AND HER CHILDREN	Bertolt Brecht	£6.99
☐ THE CHERRY ORCHARD	Anton Chekhov	£5.99
☐ TOP GIRLS	Caryl Churchill	£6.99
☐ A TASTE OF HONEY	Shelagh Delaney	£6.99
☐ STRIFE	John Galsworthy	£5.99
☐ ACROSS OKA	Robert Holman	£5.99
☐ A DOLL'S HOUSE	Henrik Ibsen	£5.99
☐ MY MOTHER SAID I NEVER SHOULD	Charlotte Keatley	£6.99
☐ DREAMS OF ANNE FRANK	Bernard Kops	£5.99
☐ BLOOD WEDDING	Federico Lorca	£5.99
☐ THE MALCONTENT	John Marston	£5.99
☐ BLOOD BROTHERS	Willy Russell	£6.99
☐ DEATH AND THE KING'S HORSEMAN	Wole Soyinka	£6.99
☐ THE PLAYBOY OF THE WESTERN WORLD	J.M. Synge	£5.99
☐ OUR COUNTRY'S GOOD	Timberlake Wertenbaker	£6.99
☐ THE IMPORTANCE OF BEING EARNEST	Oscar Wilde	£5.99
☐ A STREETCAR NAMED DESIRE	Tennessee Williams	£5.99

• All Methuen Drama books are available through mail order or from your local bookshop.

Please send cheque/eurocheque/postal order (sterling only) Access, Visa, Mastercard, Diners Card, Switch or Amex.

☐☐☐☐☐☐☐☐☐☐☐☐☐☐☐☐

Expiry Date: _____ Signature: _____

Please allow 75 pence per book for post and packing U.K.
Overseas customers please allow £1.00 per copy for post and packing.

ALL ORDERS TO:

Methuen Books, Books by Post, TBS Limited, The Book Service, Colchester Road, Frating Green, Colchester, Essex CO7 7DW.

NAME: _____

ADDRESS: _____

_____

_____

Please allow 28 days for delivery. Please tick box if you do not
wish to receive any additional information ☐

Prices and availability subject to change without notice.

Companies, institutions and other organisations wishing to make bulk purchases of any Methuen Drama books should contact their local bookseller or Metheun direct: Methuen Drama, 215 Vauxhall Bridge Road, London SW1V 1EJ. Tel: 020 7798 1600; Fax: 020 7828 2098. For a FREE Methuen Drama catalogue please contact Methuen Drama at the above address.